Romance AND Realism

CHRISTOPHER CAUDWELL wa[s] pseudonym of Christopher St. [John] Sprigg, a British journalist [and] professional writer who becar[e an] important philosopher and cri[tic in] the 1930's, author of *Illusion and Reality* and *Studies in a Dying Culture.*

In the mid-thirties Caudwell joined the Communist Party; he died in 1937 in the defense of Madrid, leaving the manuscript of *Romance and Realism* unpublished. This short but comprehensive book is a Marxist interpretation of English literature from Shakespeare to Spender. The author follows the course of English history—from the end of feudalism through the age of exploration, the rise of the common man, industrialization, science—producing his particular synthesis of literature as a subjective experience (romance) and as a response to society (realism). The major writers and movements of English literature are discussed, often with brilliant observations.

Romance and Realism is important as Marxist criticism, as a reflection of the acrid definitions of the writers of the thirties (including Auden, Orwell, C. Day Lewis), and as the highly personal view of a talented critic.

Samuel Hynes, author of *The Edwardian Turn of Mind*, has written a critical introduction about this essay and Caudwell's place in English letters.

Romance AND Realism

A STUDY IN ENGLISH
BOURGEOIS LITERATURE

$\mathcal{R}$omance AND Realism

A STUDY IN
ENGLISH BOURGEOIS LITERATURE

By Christopher Caudwell

Edited by Samuel Hynes

PRINCETON UNIVERSITY PRESS

Princeton, New Jersey

1970

Introduction

By Samuel Hynes

INTRODUCTION

I.

THE MARXIST critic Georg Lukács said of one of his books that it had been written as a polemic, but might soon "acquire the character of an historical document."[1] If history is yesterday's polemics, then the works of Christopher Caudwell are historical documents: their meaning and value for us lie partly in their relation to an historical moment, and to a generation. They belong to the 1930's, and to that generation of young writers—Auden and Spender, Isherwood, Orwell, Day Lewis, Greene—who through their writings helped to give the period its acrid definition.

In the shaping of the young men of the Thirties, two influences seem most important: the First World War, which they were old enough to know but too young to fight in, and the mood of the post-war decade during which they came of age. The literature of the war has made us aware of the effect it had on those who fought —we read Wilfred Owen as history—but we know less about what happened to boys who saw their fathers and brothers go to war, and who were left behind with the rationing and the home-front cant. "I do not claim to discern how deeply the iron has entered into the souls of those who were in the nursery in 1914," Edmund Blunden wrote in 1931, "but it seems obvious that they have grown up amid unnerving conditions, and such as destroy vision."[2]

1 Georg Lukács, *The Meaning of Contemporary Realism* (London: Merlin Press, 1963), p. 8.
2 "An Institution and a Moral," *Oxford Outlook*, XI (November 1931), 191-92.

= 3 =

Of the nature of those unnerving conditions we have substantial testimony. From Auden and Day Lewis: "As for the intelligent reader, we can only remind him, where he experiences distaste, that no universalized system—political, religious, or metaphysical—has been bequeathed to us. . . ." From Isherwood: "We young writers of the middle 'twenties were all suffering, more or less subconsciously, from a feeling of shame that we hadn't been old enough to take part in the European war." From Orwell: "By 1918 everyone under forty was in a bad temper with his elders, and the mood of anti-militarism which followed naturally upon the fighting was extended into a general revolt against orthodoxy and authority. At that time there was, among the young, a curious cult of hatred of 'old men.' The dominance of 'old men' was held to be responsible for every evil known to humanity, and every accepted institution from Scott's novels to the House of Lords was derided merely because 'old men' were in favour of it." From Michael Roberts: "Sergeants of our school O.T.C.s, admirers of our elder brothers, we grew up under the shadow of war: we have no memory of pre-war prosperity and a settled Europe. To us, that tale is text-book history: Wolsey, Canute, Disraeli, Balfour. We remember only post-war booms, which even we, poets, schoolmasters, engineers, could see were doomed to sharp extinction."[3]

The end of prosperity, the shadow of war, the loss of belief—these were in the minds of the young men as they entered the Thirties. England seemed like some dying organism, helpless to treat its own sickness: the economy was slowing, factories were idle and exports declining, unemployment was increasing sharply, and

[3] Auden and Lewis, preface to *Oxford Poetry 1927* (Oxford: Basil Blackwell, 1927), p. vii; Isherwood, *Lions and Shadows* (London: Hogarth, 1938), p. 74; Roberts, preface to *New Country* (London: Hogarth, 1933), p. 9; Orwell, *The Road to Wigan Pier* (London: Gollancz, 1937), p. 170.

the pound falling, but neither the Labour government nor the coalition National government that succeeded it was equal to the crisis. To the young it seemed that institutional political methods had failed.

And while the Old Men in Parliament did nothing, or not enough, to arrest economic collapse, Europe drifted helplessly toward another war. The complex attitude of the young toward that approaching catastrophe is implicit in Isherwood's guilt, and in Orwell's hatred of the Old Men. A cynical view of the First World War made them pacifists (for example in the famous "King and Country" resolution of the Oxford Union in 1933), but as the decade wore on more and more young men felt the need to oppose the coming violence with violence (as Orwell and many others did in Spain).

The lack of a "universalized system" is less precisely demonstrable, but it was pervasive; it underlies what most distinguishes the Thirties as a literary and intellectual period: the prevailing feeling of separation from a living past. One finds this feeling in Auden's poems, in Graham Greene's entertainments, in period movements like Mass Observation and Surrealism, in both left-wing and right-wing politics. The past is there as a clutter of dead and useless rubbish, or as the repressive weapons of the Old Men, or as a lost record to be rediscovered and reinterpreted, but it is not a vital force.

All these factors—social and intellectual, factual and emotional—together compose the special feeling that the decade of the Thirties had for the young men who lived through it: of a unique point in history, disintegrating and apocalyptic, a beginning, perhaps, but certainly an end of everything exhausted and familiar.

Caudwell called it "a dying culture"; like others of his generation he felt the crisis acutely as a crisis of belief, more strongly, perhaps, because he had been raised as a Roman Catholic. Disintegration was a characteristic of his generation, he said, and he recognized the need for a faith to replace what had been lost. In an unpublished story that Caudwell admitted was autobiographical, the principal character says: "We both need a religion, but what religions are there to have nowadays? Communism remains, I suppose. . . ." This notion of Communism, as a surrogate religion, explains a good deal about Caudwell, but it explains more about his time. It explains why *conversion* is the right word for the commitments of the young in the Thirties to Marxism, and why both the Church and the Party had their successes. It suggests a way of dealing with the obscurities of *The Orators* and the heresies of *The Road to Wigan Pier*. And it suggests that the young in the Thirties were more often motivated by the will-to-believe than by the will-to-change the world.

II

"CHRISTOPHER CAUDWELL" was the pseudonym of Christopher St. John Sprigg, an energetic and prolific journalist who was just beginning to make a reputation as a popular writer when he died in 1937. He was born in 1907 (the same year as Auden), and was educated at a Benedictine school near London, but left school at fifteen to become a reporter on the *Yorkshire Observer*, where his father was literary editor, and never went back (he used to say that he learned everything he knew from the London Library). In 1925 he moved to London to join his brother, an editor and publisher of aviation journals, and for the rest of his life made his living as a professional writer, using his own name. The career of "Christopher Caudwell" was almost entirely posthumous; the only book published under that name during his lifetime was his one serious novel, *This My Hand* (1936). Caudwell seemed to want to separate his existence as a journalist from his existence as an artist and thinker; in the end, death made the separation, for all the important books published since his death were published under the pseudonym, and Caudwell became known when Sprigg was dead.[4]

All those important books were also written after Caudwell became a Marxist. The conversion, when it came, was complete, but it was late in coming. Caudwell's life up to 1935 seems to have been quite apolitical. Because he did not go to a university, he did not meet the young intellectuals who were developing their social and political consciences after 1930;[5] he apparently never met any member of the Auden-Spender group, nor any other literary Marxist, for that matter. This was not, I think, intentional; Caudwell's life simply did not touch the lives of the smart literary Left. He was a writer all his adult life, but his was a journalist's career, and, although he always felt his true vocation to be poetry, he published only one poem

[4] These biographical details are drawn from the note written for Caudwell's *Poems* by his close friend Paul Beard, from conversations with Caudwell's brother, and from unpublished family papers. A full-length biography of Caudwell, by Mr. George Moberg, is near completion.

[5] The emergence of left-wing politics at the universities can be dated fairly precisely in student magazines. The *Oxford Outlook*, which had been an aesthetical-literary journal, turned radically political in its May 1932 issue, and *Cambridge Left* first appeared in summer 1933. See also Julian Bell's letter to the *New Statesman*, Dec. 9, 1933, pp. 731-32, in which he wrote: "In the Cambridge that I first knew, in 1929 and 1930, the central subject of ordinary conversation was poetry. As far as I can remember we hardly ever talked or thought about politics. . . . By the end of 1933, we have arrived at a situation in which almost the only subject of discussion is contemporary politics, and in which a very large majority of the more intelligent undergraduates are Communists, or almost Communists."

during his lifetime,[6] and was totally unknown as a poet.

From 1925 until the end of 1936 Caudwell worked as a journalist, edited trade papers, acted as a press agent, and wrote a number of books. He was a rapid and prolific writer; during the last five years of his life, from his twenty-fourth birthday until he died at twenty-nine, he wrote seven crime novels, five books on flying, a serious novel (*This My Hand*), *Illusion and Reality*, the thirteen essays included in *Studies in a Dying Culture* and *Further Studies*, and enough poems for a small volume. During one three-month period in 1934, while working four half-days a week in an office, he wrote a detective novel, a textbook on aviation, thirty articles on flying, six short stories, and a number of poems. In addition to his published works, he left a mass of unpublished manuscripts: a book of aphorisms in the manner of Nietzsche, two booklength collections of stories, three plays, a mock epic on the Anglo-German Naval Agreement, and two additional studies, of which this book is one.

Nearly half of Caudwell's published prose writings (twelve books in all) are concerned with crime and flying, activities that in retrospect seem peculiarly expressive of the time. The Thirties was the period of the flowering of English crime fiction, and also of the great adventurous flights, and the Detective and the Airman are figures that recur in popular literature, films, and the daily press. The fiction of crime and its detection is obviously appropriate to a time conscious of the lack of "universalized systems" and of the breakdown of social order; it offers escape into a simplified moral world. Flying is another kind of escape; it is

6 The one poem was "Once Did I Think," published under his own name, Christopher Sprigg, in the *Dial*, vol. 82 (March 1927), 187. The editor of the magazine at that time was Marianne Moore.

individual and skillful, and, in its purest form, like other arts, is perfectly useless. Caudwell, in his *Great Flights*, a popular history of long-distance flying, justified his subject thus: "It is unnecessary to answer the practical man; for the value of long-distance flying is not practical, any more than is that of exploring, sport, or mountaineering. All have values that are higher than the merely practical. The justification of long-distance flying is its demonstration of human courage and skill battling against the dangers of a still unknown element."[7] In these terms, the Airman is an epic hero. One can see the appeal of such a man of action, at once simple and valuable, in a time of depression and uncertainty; the same needs lay behind the curious apotheosizing of T. E. Lawrence after his death in 1935. To men of the Thirties like Caudwell, the Communist must have seemed another such hero —a man of action in a passive, paralyzed time, risking the cautious securities of life in an epic cause.

One other strain in Caudwell's writings is worth noting. Among his unpublished work is a book of short stories, written in imitation of Kafka during the winter of 1934-1935. They are not very good stories, as Caudwell realized, but they connect him with the strain of allegory that runs through much English writing of the Thirties and is most brilliantly realized in the novels of Rex Warner and in the poems and plays of Auden. To some degree Caudwell was no doubt simply imitating a current fashion (the Muir translations of Kafka began to appear in England in 1930), but he was also expressing an impulse of his time, the impulse to shape experience in a way that would not violate its incomprehensible disorder. Kafka-esque allegory is a desperate kind of myth-making, and it is not surprising that Caudwell, with his sense of the need for a new religion, should respond to it.

[7] *Great Flights* (London: Thos. Nelson & Sons, 1935), p. 3.

= 9 =

In all these ways Caudwell was clearly in sympathetic touch with the spirit of the Thirties before he turned to Communism, though that commitment was also a common gesture of the time. Toward the end of 1934 he began to be absorbed in Marxism, and by the next summer he must have had a fair knowledge of the Marxist classics; the bibliography of *Illusion and Reality*, which he was writing then, includes basic works by Marx and Engels, Lenin, Bukharin, Plekhanov, and Stalin. He does not seem to have been influenced in his political thinking by any personal acquaintance; like Bunyan, he was converted by the study of Holy Writ alone.

It was during this period of conversion that Caudwell began a book that at first he called *Verse and Mathematics—a Study of the Foundation of Poetry*. To write it he moved for the summer to Porthleven, in Cornwall, and by July he was halfway through a first draft, and writing at the rate of five thousand words a day. He finished the draft in September, and mailed the manuscript—by then called *Illusion and Reality*— to a friend for a critical reading. By November the book was under consideration at Allen & Unwin; it was rejected, and later was submitted to Macmillan, where it was accepted. In the interim between submissions, Caudwell may have revised his manuscript, but he cannot have expanded it much; his word count of the first draft—120,000 words—is roughly the length of the published version. The book was published in the spring of 1937, shortly after Caudwell's death.

Illusion and Reality is not, then, the work of a Communist Party member, but rather of a poet who felt himself drawn and persuaded by Marxist theory. Caudwell's motive in writing the book, it seems clear, was to work out the implications for poetry of the doctrine that he was then discovering. Only the last chapter, "The Future of Poetry," seems doctrinaire, and that, I would guess, is his principal later addition to the original manuscript.

When he had completed the book, Caudwell returned to London and settled in Poplar, a working-class district near the East London docks. His reason for doing so is explicitly set out in the unpublished story from which I quoted above: "We both need a religion, but what religions are there nowadays? Communism remains, I suppose, but before I can embrace that I must go down, down to the depths, and be one of what a Communist must believe alone has the right to exist to-day, the anonymous proletariat." At first glance this seems very like the impulse that ten years earlier had sent George Orwell to live among the down-and-out. "I wanted to submerge myself," Orwell wrote, "to get right down among the oppressed, to be one of them and on their side against their tyrants."[8] For Orwell, this action was an expiation of class-guilt, and his story of his descent into voluntary poverty is a confession of self-inflicted punishment. Caudwell's choice seems a good deal less neurotic: he chose to live in a settled working-class community rather than among outcasts, and he entered into the life of a part of that community by joining the local branch of the Communist Party. Perhaps most important, he did not write about it; that is, he treated his choice as life, and not as "experience."

Orwell was probably right to regard such gestures as sentimental and bound to fail; even in destitution Orwell remained an Old Etonian, and nothing that an intellectual like Caudwell could do would make him one of the anonymous proletariat. Still, it is important to note that Caudwell alone among the left-wing intellectuals of his generation was willing, to use a phrase of Lenin's that Auden was fond of quoting, "to go hungry, work illegally, and be anonymous." By join-

[8] *The Road to Wigan Pier*, p. 180.

= 11 =

ing the local branch he entered the Party not as an intellectual but as a rank-and-file member, committed to ordinary drudging Party work—bill-posting, slogan-chalking, and speaking on street corners. During the next year he spent a good deal of his time at such tasks; so far as I can tell he never mixed with the Party intelligentsia or the fashionable fellow-travellers.

It is worthwhile recalling the dates of Caudwell's Party activism; he joined the Poplar branch near the end of 1935, and worked there until December 1936. It was a good time to be a left-wing idealist: during that year Hitler occupied the Rhineland, Abyssinia fell to the Italians, and the Spanish Civil War began. In London, troops of Sir Oswald Moseley's British Union of Fascists made their most serious effort to invade the East End, and were repulsed by the workers, and the Hunger Marchers from Jarrow arrived in Westminster to confront Parliament with the plain truth of their suffering. Caudwell did not live to learn of Stalin's purges, or of the Russo-German Pact, or of the Communist betrayals of Spanish leftists. In December he drove an ambulance to Spain, and there he joined the International Brigade. On his first day of combat, February 12, 1937, he was killed in the defense of Madrid.

It was during his year in the Party that Caudwell wrote his *Studies in a Dying Culture* and *Further Studies*. In a letter of November 1935, just at the time of his move to Poplar, Caudwell remarked that the book was taking shape, and he sketched a table of contents that is roughly the contents of the two published volumes. By the end of April 1936 a first draft was finished, and Caudwell was beginning to revise. He went on writing and revising through the summer and autumn, adding to one of the essays, on physics, until it grew into a separate book; it was published posthumously as *The Crisis in Physics*. By December, when Caudwell left for Spain, he had shown a version of *Studies* to his friends, but he considered the book still unfinished.

Caudwell's reason for writing the *Studies* was, I think, essentially the same as his reason for joining the Party. In November 1935, when he was living in Poplar but had not yet become a Party member, Caudwell wrote a self-analyzing letter to his friends Paul and Betty Beard, in which he said:

"Seriously, I think my weakness has been the lack ' of an integrated Weltanschauung. I mean one that includes my emotional, scientific, and artistic needs. They have been more than usually disintegrated in me, I think, a characteristic of my generation exacerbated by the fact that, as you know, I have strong rationalising as well as artistic tendencies. As long as there was a disintegration I had necessarily an unsafe provisional attitude to reality, a somewhat academic superficial attitude, which showed in my writing as what Betty has described as the 'lack of baking.' The remedy is nothing so simple as a working-over and polishing-up of prose, but to come to terms with myself and my environment. This I think during the last year or two I have begun to do. Naturally it is a long process (the getting of wisdom) and I don't fancy I am anywhere near the end. But 'I and R.' represented a milestone on the way, and that, I think, was why it seemed sincere, free from my other faults, and, with its necessary limitations, successful."

This need for a Weltanschauung, which Caudwell rightly saw as characteristic of his generation, led him to Marxism, and to the ambitious effort to apply Marxist methods of analysis to the widest possible range of intellectual problems.

As an epigraph for *Studies in a Dying Culture*, Caudwell planned to use a quotation from Lenin: "Communism becomes an empty phrase, a mere façade, and the Communist a mere bluffer, if he has not worked over in his consciousness the whole inheritance of human knowledge." The quotation does not appear in either of the *Studies* volumes, but it remains highly appropriate to Caudwell's intentions. Caudwell believed that such an applied ideology was necessary to modern thought, and he criticized major modern figures who lacked it. The weakness of Freudian psychology he took to be "the lack of any synthetic world-view in which to fit the empirical discoveries made,"[9] and he thought H. G. Wells was muddled in his thought because "he was devoid of any world-view and had not escaped from the inborn bewilderment of the *petit bourgeois*. . . ."[10] He intended his *Studies* to compose such a world-view, the "whole inheritance of human knowledge" worked over by one Marxist consciousness. When one considers the circumstances in which he wrote, and the time he had, it is astonishing that he came as close as he did to fulfilling that intention. In the space of about a year, while he was heavily engaged in Party activities and was supporting himself as a writer, he managed to draft essays on the Superman, the Hero, the Artist, Utopianism, ethics, love, psychology, liberty, religion, aesthetics, history, physics, English literature, and biology. (Of these only the last remains unpublished.) These essays, even in their unfinished state, compose a document that is the best synthetic account we have of English Marxist thought in the mid-Thirties. The essays on literature and literary figures, together with *Illusion and Reality*, are certainly the most important Marxist criticism in English.

III

SERIOUS MARXIST literary criticism did not appear in England until well on into the 1930's. We tend to think

[9] *Illusion and Reality*, p. 159.
[10] *Studies in a Dying Culture* (London: The Bodley Head, 1938), p. 83.

= 14 =

of the intellectuals of that decade as having a single political inclination, but in fact the swing to the Left was hesitant and slow. It was obvious from the beginning of the Thirties that western civilization was undergoing an unprecedented crisis—economic collapse, the rise of fascism, the failure of liberal leadership, the threat of war—but it was less obvious how intellectuals should respond to the crisis. Auden, in a birthday poem to Isherwood, asked him to "make action urgent and its nature clear";[11] but in fact only the urgency was clear. Communism existed as a possible choice, but an uncertain one; when young men like Day Lewis and Spender looked to the Left they saw a noble experiment, but they also saw "the bully and the spy," and they wondered whether the revolution was worth the cost.[12] The price of action seemed to be the loss of individual freedom and the surrender of humane values; intellectuals who felt drawn to the Party nevertheless hung back.

Before 1936 there was almost no English criticism that could seriously be called Marxist. John Strachey had published strident polemical attacks on bourgeois writers, and Philip Henderson had attempted literary history from a Marxist point of view,[13] but neither had got beyond partisanship to critical theory. The major works of English Marxist criticism belong to the first year of the Spanish Civil War. Caudwell's *Illusion and Reality*, Alick West's *Crisis and Criticism*, and Ralph Fox's *The Novel and the People* were all published early in 1937 (by the time they appeared Caudwell and Fox were dead in Spain). This is also the period

11 W. H. Auden, *Look, Stranger!* (London: Faber: 1936), p. 66.
12 Stephen Spender, *World Within World* (London: Hamish Hamilton, 1951), p. 202; Lewis, *A Hope for Poetry* (Oxford: Blackwell, 1934), p. 47.
13 John Strachey, *Literature and Dialectical Materialism* (New York: Covici, Friede, 1934); Philip Henderson, *Literature and a Changing Civilisation* (London: Bodley Head, 1935).

= 15 =

of two other important Left books, Spender's *Forward from Liberalism* and Orwell's *The Road to Wigan Pier*, which, though they did not please orthodox Communists, did attract intellectuals to the Left.

The best theoretical books appeared at this time, I think, because the crisis had taken active and violent form; clarification of the issues in other terms became both possible and important. For some men, the urgency was also personal; certainly Caudwell went to Spain aware that he might die there. He left his work in publishable drafts, with instructions for dealing with them in the event that he was killed. But, most fundamentally, the Spanish war changed the climate of the Thirties by turning the crisis into a cause, and making action unavoidable. One of the consequences, though it may seem paradoxical, was that for a brief period English Marxist criticism became more than partisan; it became profound.

When Caudwell began to write *Illusion and Reality* in 1935, he had no English tradition of Marxist criticism on which to build; he was starting out alone—his isolation in Cornwall was an appropriate gesture—to construct his own theory. Nor did the Marxist classics that he was reading provide an aesthetic theory; Marx and Engels offered at most hints as to what such a theory might include. From Marx, Caudwell took two key ideas. From the introduction to the *Critique of Political Economy*: "The mode of production of the material means of life determines, in general, the social, political, and intellectual processes of life. It is not the consciousness of human beings which determines their existence, it is their social existence which determines their consciousness." And from the *Theses on Feuerbach*: "The philosophers have only *interpreted* the world in various ways: the point, however, is to *change* it."

The first of these quotations implies a theory of the *sources* of literary subjects and attitudes: literature is a social activity, a mode of action with its bases in the modes of production; consciousness, including literary consciousness, is determined by the conditions of existence. Caudwell set the passage, in a somewhat longer context, as the epigraph to one of his *Studies*. The second quotation implies a theory of the *function* of literature: literature, like other ideological forms, is an arena in which men fight out their conflicts, and so change the world. Caudwell used this remark as the concluding sentence of Chapter IX of *Illusion and Reality*, and in his essay on "Reality" in *Further Studies*. Taken together, the two quotations provided him with an authoritative base for his own theory of literature.

To these ideas, Caudwell added others, of which the most important derives from a sentence of Engels that he set as the epigraph to *Illusion and Reality*: "Freedom is the recognition of necessity." As Caudwell applies this idea to the relation between man and his literature, it makes of literature an individual, liberating force, a mode of knowledge rather than of action, to be understood in terms of consciousness rather than of social existence, as for example in this passage: "The phantasy of art, by the constant changes in organisation which it produces in man's ego, makes man conscious of the necessity of his instincts and therefore free."[14] Caudwell sums up this view of the role of literature in the final sentence of *Illusion and Reality*: "Art is one of the conditions of man's realisation of himself, and in its turn is one of the realities of man."[15]

Caudwell's intention in this line of argument seems to have been to find a way of treating literature in Marxist terms that would preserve the idea that literature was intrinsically valuable to the individual, and

[14] *Illusion and Reality*, p. 190.
[15] *Illusion and Reality*, p. 298.

would make art more than an instrument of social change. Particularly in the second half of *Illusion and Reality*, where he discusses the relation of poetry to dream, phantasy, and illusion, the effect is to separate poetry from direct contact with the objective world of action and to relate it to personal, subjective experience, "the inner world of feelings." There is little here about art's role in changing the world; Caudwell did not see the revolutionary function of art as crucial, and many of his most direct statements about the relation of art to the individual seem ambiguous on the point of action. For example: "Art adapts the psyche to the environment, and is therefore one of the conditions of the development of society." "A great novel is how we should like our own lives to be, not petty or dull, but full of great issues, turning even death to a noble sound. . . ." "Art tells us the significance and meaning of all we are in the language of feeling. . . ."[16] It seems to me that all of these allow a reading of art as individual and inward, though a Marxist might read them in another way.

It is not strange that a man who thought of himself always as a poet should urge the value of his vocation in individual, human terms. But Caudwell was also a philosopher, concerned to define a synthetic worldview, and one of his strengths was his ability to make synthesizing connections between areas of thought. *Illusion and Reality* is a study of the sources of poetry, but it draws its substance primarily from non-poetical fields; the bibliography contains over 500 titles, but only five are books of poetry—T. S. Eliot's *Poems*, Apollinaire's *Alcools*, and three volumes of translations from the Chinese. The study of poetry's sources, as Caudwell says in his introduction, cannot be separated from the study of society: ". . . but physics, anthropology, history, biology, philosophy and psychol-

16 *Illusion and Reality*, pp. 261, 262, 263.

ogy are also products of society, and therefore a sound sociology would enable the art critic to employ criteria drawn from those fields without falling into eclecticism or confusing art with psychology or politics."[17] Caudwell could see implications for art in Heisenberg's Principle of Indeterminacy, and connections between Fascist art and the psychology of neurotic regression, and he felt that the intellectual situation of his time required that such connections be made. He spelled out the problem as he saw it in this passage from *Illusion and Reality*:

"This dichotomy between life and the most valued function is only possible because the development of bourgeois culture has produced a flying apart of all ideology into separate spheres of art, philosophy, physics, psychology, history, biology, economics, music, anthropology and the like which, as they increase their internal organisation and achievement, mutually repel each other and increase the general confusion. This is merely an equivalent in the field of thought of the way in which organisation within the factory has increased disorganisation between the factory; it is the struggle of productive forces with productive relations; it is the quarrel of real elements with bourgeois categories; it is part of the basic contradiction of capitalism. The task of the proletariat is just as much to integrate this ideological confusion and raise it to a new level of consciousness, as it is to integrate the economic confusion and raise it to a new level of production. One task is the counterpart of the other, and both have a common aim—to win more freedom for humanity."[18]

This effort to integrate the ideological confusion of the time determined the method of everything theoretical that Caudwell wrote (for example in the passage

17 *Illusion and Reality*, pp. 11-12.
18 *Illusion and Reality*, p. 287.

just quoted, in the relation made between the "field of thought" and factory organization); it is evident in the variety of sources that he used for *Illusion and Reality*, and in the extraordinary range of his *Studies*. Communism appealed to him because it offered a consistent world-view, in terms of which the anarchy of modern thought could be synthesized. One might say that he became a Communist in order to see bourgeois culture clearly.

It may be this synthesizing quality that has made Caudwell so difficult to deal with, and has made appreciation of his work slow in coming. Some reviewers recognized the importance of the books as they appeared—Auden wrote of *Illusion and Reality* that it was "the most important book on poetry since the books of Dr. Richards," and J.B.S. Haldane thought that if Caudwell had lived to complete *The Crisis in Physics* it "might have been one of the most important books of our time."[19] But there was no serious discussion of Caudwell's ideas until after the Second World War. In 1948 two essays appeared: Stanley Edgar Hyman's chapter on Caudwell and Marxist criticism in *The Armed Vision*, and Alick West's "On 'Illusion and Reality'" in *The Communist Review*.[20] Both are valuable introductions to Caudwell, summarizing his ideas in a useful way for audiences that did not know them. But in 1948 *Further Studies* had not been published, and Caudwell was so little known that not much beyond an introduction was possible.

The first extended commentary on Caudwell was a series of critiques by British Marxists that appeared in *Modern Quarterly* in 1951. This "Caudwell Discussion," as it came to be called, ran through an entire

[19] Auden, in *New Verse*, 25 (May 1937), 22; Haldane, in *Labour Monthly*, 21 (August 1939), 509.
[20] Hyman, *The Armed Vision* (New York: Knopf, 1948); West, *Communist Review* (January 1948), 7-13.

= 20 =

year's issues, with contributions from fourteen crit-ics.[21] It began with a sharp attack on Caudwell's ortho-doxy, which was vigorously refuted in the next issue, and throughout the controversy pro- and anti-Caud-well opinions remained strong and irreconcilable. Caudwell's detractors attacked that aspect of his the-ory that turns from art as a reflection of reality to art as subjective experience: he had not thrown off his bourgeois background; his theory of poetry in-volved concepts—the instincts, irrationalism, the "in-ner world"—that showed the influence of bourgeois psychology and biology; he was guilty of false antith-eses (between nature and society, said one critic; be-tween perception and thought, said another); he was constructing a theory of "pure poetry," which is a bourgeois theory; his idea of poetry's "dream work" was a romantic idea and led away from socialist real-ism. "Whatever all this may be," wrote Maurice Corn-forth, "it is certainly not Marxism."

To a non-Marxist, Cornforth's conclusion does not seem very damning, and most of the charges brought against Caudwell by other Marxists seem simply de-scriptive of what he indeed had said. It is true that in *Illusion and Reality* he found the roots of poetry, both historically and individually, in the primitive and the instinctual. It is true that his views of the function of art in society owe much to Freud. And it is true that his idea of lyric poetry is in the Romantic tradition. No doubt it was a weakness of his theorizing that he found it difficult to reconcile that Romantic idea with

[21] Maurice Cornforth, "Caudwell and Marxism," *Modern Quarterly*, VI, 1 (Winter 1950-51), 16-33; George Thomson, "In Defence of Poetry," VI, 2 (Spring 1951), 107-34; "The Caud-well Discussion," contributions by Alan Bush, Montagu Slater, Alick West, G. M. Mathews, Jack Beeching, Peter Cronin, VI, 3 (Summer 1951), 259-75; "The Caudwell Discussion," contribu-tions by Margot Heinemann, Edward York, Werner Thierry, G. Robb, J. D. Bernal, Edwin S. Smith, Maurice Cornforth, VI, 4 (Autumn 1951), 340-58.

his political ideology. But one must conclude that most of the hostile contributions to the "Caudwell Discussion" call into question his "correctness" as a Marxist, not his contributions as a critic and thinker.

One criticism must be taken more seriously, because it comes from a man who was both a distinguished scientist and one of the most brilliant of British Marxists. J. D. Bernal criticized Caudwell savagely, and some of his objections are shrewdly noted. Bernal observed that Caudwell's scientific essays appealed mainly to literary intellectuals, for whom scientific rigor is impossible and who are impressed by the apparent ease of Caudwell's syntheses; that Caudwell took from Einstein not the pure science, but the dubious philosophy; that he was mechanistic and overformal in his use of antithesis; that he was lacking in historical sense. This is a description of a very imperfect Marxist; but for our purposes it is more important to note that Bernal had also described an imperfect synthesizer. The latter judgment is certainly valid. Caudwell was a young man in a hurry, a self-educated polymath who was attempting an "integration of ideological confusion" that was probably beyond the powers of any one person. One might add that he was using as his synthesizing instrument a system of thought that invites antithetical constructions and reduces complexities to contradictions. It is hard to see how he could have done better than he did.

That he nevertheless did well, and that he remains a critic worthy of serious study, we may infer from the attention given his work by the greatest of Marxist critics, Georg Lukács. Caudwell is discussed in many places in Lukács' writings,[22] and the references are admiring and respectful—"the highly gifted English aesthetician," "spirited and progressive," "discerning philosopher"—even when, as is often the case, Lukács

[22] Georg Lukács, *Werke*, 12 vols. (Neuwied & Berlin, 1969), vol. 10, pp. 768-69; vol. 11, 267-68, 598, 785.

is disagreeing with a particular idea. Lukács criticizes in Caudwell the strain of romantic subjectivity that the *Modern Quarterly* critics had also noted: the magical theory of inspiration, the idea of the lyric as a withdrawal from the world, the primitivism, the subjective theory of rhythm. But he is also at pains to note, as the *Modern Quarterly* critics sometimes were not, that much of Caudwell's theory was acute and well-justified.

Caudwell's reputation as a critic remains insecure. To many Marxists he is an example of "uncorrectness," a clever young man tainted by bourgeois notions. Non-Marxists tend to regard him as a representative of "Marxist criticism," a system that to them is by definition restrictive and distorting. In either case, praise is grudging and qualified. Caudwell will get his due when he is seen as what he was—a gifted synthesizer who derived his world-view from Marx, but who was in practice heterodox and individual. (The same could be said of Lukács.) The elements of his critical thought that are, from a Marxist point of view, heresies may from a less rigid position seem original and suggestive, while his gift for relating ideas among fields, which owes much to Marxism, must strike less synthesizing minds as exceptional and valuable.[23]

IV

THOUGH CAUDWELL's reputation is principally as a critic, there is little in his published works that one could strictly call literary criticism. Some of the *Studies* are ostensibly concerned with literary men, but they compose a Marxist typology of bourgeois errors

[23] For the most recent Marxist commentary on Caudwell, see David N. Margolies, *The Function of Literature: a Study of Christopher Caudwell's Aesthetics* (New York: International Publishers, 1969). Margolies is pro-Caudwell, and sees him as "perhaps the first critic to take a fully social and fully Marxist view of art."

rather than a set of literary studies. Caudwell chose literary examples because he was himself a poet and novelist, but his Shaw is a bad Socialist, his D. H. Lawrence a failed bourgeois revolutionary, and his Wells a bourgeois Utopian. The emphasis is on their typical failures as thinkers, not on their achievements as artists. And though the three chapters on English poetry in *Illusion and Reality* treat the subject historically, and mention many names, they are very general, and tell us more about the decline of capitalism than about the growth of English poetry. It is significant that Caudwell quotes almost no verse in these chapters except Marx's favorite passage on gold from *Timon of Athens*. There is some justification, then, for the hostile judgments that some of Caudwell's critics have made—for example, Raymond Williams' remarks that Caudwell "has little to say, of actual literature, that is even interesting," and that "for the most part his discussion is not even specific enough to be wrong."[24]

This level of generality, which Williams so disliked, is simply a reflection of the way Caudwell's mind worked. He was a philosopher and aesthetician before he was a literary critic, and he was more interested in theory than in the close examination of empirical examples. No doubt his Marxism was also a factor in his generalizations, in that it encouraged him to synthesize and to see works of literature in their large social relationships. On the other hand, other Marxists have written excellent analytical criticism (Lukács is an example), and there is nothing in Marxist theory against it. Caudwell did not choose analytic criticism because the task he had set himself was to synthesize.

Caudwell acknowledged this point by making his only essay on literature a part of his synthetic study of bourgeois culture; *Romance and Realism* is far more

[24] Raymond Williams, *Culture and Society 1780-1950* (New York: Columbia University Press, 1958), p. 277.

concerned with literature than any other of Caudwell's writings, but like the other studies it sets its subject in relation to the general movement of society. "It is the bourgeois error," Caudwell wrote, "to believe in the existence of self-determined spheres of phenomena," and when he deals with literary phenomena it is with an awareness that other related spheres exist. In *Romance and Realism* he discusses English literature since Shakespeare, but always in terms of relationships—literature and history, literature and physics, and, most fundamentally, literature and economics. What he has written is a *Sociology* of English literature. The essay is organized chronologically, but it is not literary history in the traditional sense of a record of strictly literary causes and effects. Caudwell would not have thought such a record either true or useful, and his own account gives a broader sense of the movement of literature through its historical environment, flowing and being shaped, like a river in its bed.

Caudwell described his intention in writing *Romance and Realism* as "the tracing of those chief social changes which produced change in the form and technique of the novel and poetry." The development of this relationship between literary *form* and *social change* is his most original contribution to criticism in the essay. It made it possible for him to maintain the sense of a literary work as a verbal as well as a social event, and to select his examples for their formal importance rather than simply for their sociological significance. His account of the 17th century is faithful to the complexity of the time because he treats the bourgeois revolution in terms of its implications for poetic diction, and his analysis of the "epistemological crisis" at the end of the 19th century makes a persuasive case for the relation between new thought in physics and the form of the novel.

Nevertheless, the lack of historical sense that Bernal deplored in Caudwell is still evident, and still a flaw. His account of the rise of the Tudors is not likely to satisfy historians, nor is his identification of *Puritan* with *petty bourgeois*. He is weak on the economics of the Elizabethan theater, and on the decline of patronage in the 18th century; in general, his command of earlier English literature is uncertain. Other weaknesses in the essay are more directly related to Caudwell's Marxism, and may seem, to a non-Marxist, the kinds of lapses that a Marxist critic is particularly prone to. For example, there is the imbalance of treatment by which Kipling, because he represents bourgeois imperialism at an interesting stage, gets more attention than any other novelist (though less for his fiction than for his imperial context), while George Eliot is dismissed in a paragraph. I am bothered also by the way Caudwell turns even the most personal poetry into social generalization (*In Memoriam* "shows how rapidly the industrial petty bourgeois class has started to decay"). In his discussion of Hardy, Caudwell comments that "the novel is the great medium of acceptance of social relations." Perhaps for that reason Caudwell is more at ease with, and has more interesting things to say about novels than about poems, and is clumsy and perfunctory when talking about lyric poetry.

Finally there is Caudwell's style, which has distressed even his admirers. Herbert Read said that it seemed to have been inspired by bad translations of Marx,[25] and while that criticism seems too strong for *Romance and Realism*, the writing here certainly does not move with much grace. This may be in part a consequence of haste, but it is also surely connected with the need to use certain terms too often, and with the temptation to lapse into polemic.

[25] In his review of *Studies in a Dying Culture, Purpose,* XI (April-June 1939), 124.

Still, when everything negative has been said, *Romance and Realism* has ample justifying merits. The second half of the essay in particular, covering the modern literature that Caudwell knew best, is full of brilliant insights. In the section on Hardy, for example, where Caudwell could expand and linger over material that he obviously admired, and where the relation between the works and the world is crucial, his sociological method richly confirms its value to criticism. And there are many other parts that might be cited; the dismissal of Galsworthy, the appreciation of Moore's later novels, the consideration of the Auden group all demonstrate a fine critical intelligence at work.

Romance and Realism has become an historical document, and we will scarcely understand it except in relation to its time. It is Marxist criticism, from the only decade when Marxism in England engaged the best literary minds. It is touched by a common sense of urgency and crisis, and by the will to believe in a Marxist solution. Insofar as it urges a Marxist view of literature as a part of the total world-view that Caudwell believed necessary to human freedom, it is polemical; but it is unlike much Marxist writing of the time in that it is not topical, or programmatical, or incendiary. It does not damn bourgeois literature; it does not predict a golden age of literature in a classless society; it does not exhort poets to write proletarian poems. It is simply the application of a theory to a movement in society, and, because it is, it is more than *merely* an historical document. Other Marxist criticism of the Thirties seems shrill, naïve, and dated; Caudwell has something of all these qualities, but he has more. He had an exceptional mind, and he had trained himself in Marxist theory. He had worked out, far more than any other literary Marxist of his time, the implications of his convictions.

Caudwell said of the Auden group that "they have not transformed, sifted, and synthesised all bourgeois culture, physics, psychology, ethics and history into a communist world-view." Caudwell had tried to do all of that. If his account of the movement of English literature remains credible and instructive, long after the mood of the Thirties has become history, it is partly because it stands in the fuller synthesis of the *Studies*, and draws authority from the world-view of an extraordinary, learned, and brilliant young man.

Romance AND Realism

A STUDY IN ENGLISH
BOURGEOIS LITERATURE

A NOTE ON THE TEXT

THE TEXT of *Romance and Realism* is taken directly from the original typescript which, with Caudwell's other unpublished writings, is in the possession of Mr. T. Stanhope Sprigg, Caudwell's brother. The typescript is a fairly clean one, and has been copyedited in Caudwell's hand. It would no doubt have been further revised before publication, and some of the rough spots —the verbal errors and minor slips in grammar and spelling—would have been corrected, but the essays seem finished in all but these small particulars. I have confined my editing to the correction of obvious mistakes and to the insertion of a few explanatory footnotes.

S.H.

ROMANCE AND REALISM

A Study in English Bourgeois Literature

THROUGHOUT the history of bourgeois literature there is an emergence of opposites. At first glance it seems as if throughout literature two schools of thought were waging war: first one succeeds, and then the other gains the ascendancy. At the close of the 18th and the beginning of the 19th century, there is the struggle between classicists and romanticists; but as the romantic "revolution" draws to a close, this now expresses itself as a struggle between romanticism and realism. Yet realism itself, in the beginning of the 20th century, is challenged by its opposite, futurism. In fact, however, each of these opposites is a new "school"; they are not the product of an underlying dualism in the human mind. It is true that development occurs by the antagonism and synthesis of opposites in life, thought, and literature; but the opposites continually produced and reconciled by this dialectic movement are not reflections of eternal underlying opposites. This is the view of those who try to separate all the complexities of human thought into Platonism or Aristoteleanism, realism or nominalism, extraversion or introversion, romanticism or classicism, tough-mindedness or tender-mindedness. The simplest differences in literature are more complex than this elementary dualism.

The "classical" school of the 18th century, representing "reason," deism, scepticism, and materialism, is negated by romanticism, representing "feeling," occult-

= 31 =

ism, belief, and idealistic philosophy. These opposites are synthesised in "realism," in which the very wildness of romanticism, as in Flaubert's exotic *Salammbô*, Zola's extravagant bestiality, or Tolstoi's surging war canvas, is described coldly and objectively as if classicism, instead of denying the romantic world, were carefully describing it from outside without abandoning its classic convictions. Realism is a genuine synthesis; but this realism, describing the world objectively, more and more seems to rob the picture of romantic vigour, until finally it becomes unemotional, dead, and without virtue. Realism in turn explodes, and we have anti-realism. But, because the movement is dialectic, realism does not find itself opposed by the romanticism it negated, but by symbolism, futurism, and finally, *surréalisme*.

All this sounds remote and abstract; yet this purely formal movement of thought has a material basis. It is the result of a dialectic change below the surface in the productive forces and productive relations. Bourgeois literary critics, however, try to freeze this endless wave-like movement, to divide these melting interpenetrating opposites into two eternal schools, which are regarded as exclusive opposites. Such historians are therefore always embarrassed by the fact that these dualisms which keep turning up in bourgeois literature are so fluid: realism has affinities with romanticism, but also with classicism; a futurist has realist as well as romantic traits; an author seems first clearly one thing and then, looked at from another angle, is seen to be another. Nothing is simple and distinct.

This difficulty with bourgeois literature arises because the historian is himself a bourgeois. As long as he moves within the circle of bourgeois categories, such opposites as he finds there seem absolute and complete; but we, if we look at this world from outside, should be able to see that, far from being absolute and complete, these bourgeois opposites are both generated by the fundamental bourgeois position. They are aspects of reality extracted by the same machine, and are almost like the negative and positive of one photographic process. If one had seen only one photograph of reality, its negative and positive would indeed seem to be eternal opposites. But if one had seen others, one would have seen that really there was not much to choose between the negative and positive taken from one aspect. The real difference arises when one photographs from *different points.*

Although the bourgeois is always trying to reduce the literary process to simple opposites of this nature, he is perpetually defeated by the dialectic nature of art. His simple opposites overlap, not only with one series in time (romanticist over realist and realist over romanticist and futurist) but with different pairs in one author, so that, in any given era, such important opposites as objectivity and subjectivity, cynic and sentimentalist, idealist and materialist, individualist and traditionalist, vulgarian and aesthete, cross each other in the most confusing way, and the bourgeois critic can never find a fundamental pair of opposites that will, by selection, align all the others and so bring order into the confusion.

This is because every pair of opposites he selects, however seemingly fundamental, is generated by the movement below the surface of one developing thing, bourgeois social relations. As all the critics' other categories are bourgeois, he could never see this; it is like trying to look through himself; the opposites always seem to him to be exclusive and absolute. Once we penetrate to the core of the matter, to the mode of motion of bourgeois society, everything becomes clear. It is like an X-ray lighting up the bones of culture and thus showing us the simple calcerous foundation of the complex and flexible organs. Such a broad view of bourgeois English literature, however rapidly it surveys the ground, shows how moving social relations give rise to the already recognized but inexplicable changes in the art secreted by society.

What is the function of the author in society? It is his business to be an artist in words, that is, to express by means of language a peculiar experience he has had in life.

Language, experience, life, express—these four words lay down at once the framework within which the author moves.

He expresses an experience—an affective attitude towards reality—by means of language. Language is a storehouse of social experience, of symbols referring to real phenomena but expressing affective attitudes towards such phenomena. Such old social references and notions as exist are not enough for him. He has a new experience to communicate. His task, therefore, is so to recombine these symbols that out of the recombination will come a new experience nearer to his. The new combination will then express *socially* his *personal* reaction to reality.

As seen by the author, the process is that an experience A, which is part of his personal world, must be synthesised with the language world B, common to both him and his readers and therefore social, in such a way as to give rise to C, which is his new experience A, but now transformed to live in the social world B.

As seen by the reader, the process is that a new experience A^1, which is the author's C, is the antithesis to all that is contained in his language world, B, and

= 34 =

the tension of the new experience alters *his* personal world C^1 so that it now includes A^1.

As a result both parties are changed. By the author's labour in making his personal experience social and public, the experience itself is changed in quality and becomes a new experience, and the author discovers more about himself. And the reader, in striving to make this new part of the social language world personal to him, is also changed; his language world is thereafter different for him. Both author and reader, living their lives, are now themselves different, and their lives are different.

The common term, making these transformations possible, is the medium in which author and readers all live—society, which secretes the language world in which both can meet. Art therefore is a process pervading social relations, and its pattern must be woven among theirs. Social life causes the author to have certain experiences which furnish the emotions of art, and causes the reader, by reason of his experience, to have certain affective associations to words, furnishing the means by which the author's experiences are communicated to him. The experiences themselves are what they are because of the author's life. Their poignancy is given in the problem of the times. Not only the material, but also the affective heat of his art, is drawn from the social environment of the time.

This is true of all societies, however simple; but not all societies are simple, and none are the same. The differences make the operation of this process different in different ages; the complexities make the process more difficult to follow in more complex societies.

Language is not something consecrated to art. It is a medium of communication used for the business of daily life, science and politics, for securing cooperation and reciprocity among men in aim, feelings, and action. Art works in this already given material. True, artistic language is different from conversational, but it is none the less fed by it; otherwise it would be possible to have an entirely different literary language— say Esperanto—used only for art. It is well known that no art could be written in such a language, which would be poor and bare of precisely the matter art requires. This shows that all the ordinary social associations and meanings language gathers in the market place are not only useable by literary art but are essential to it. Social use furnishes the matter art requires. Nor can it be urged that art requires a literary tradition, and that Esperanto has none. If this were the case, it would be possible to produce great literature in a dead language, such as Latin or Greek, with great literary traditions. But this, too, as is well known, is impossible. The traditions of art are not language traditions, but social traditions. Literary art therefore has as an essential feature the use of associations gathered in shops, market places, friendly conversations, political speeches and quarrels. It is not surprising therefore if literary art is conditioned at every step by social relations, because it is using the product of social relationships, fabricated by the necessities of human cooperation. Its task is to work over, heighten, and make significant this product.

But what seems to art heightening and significant is also dictated by the artist's experience of life, by the adventures of the genotype in the changing social world. In a sense what interests art will be what is not already contained in social experience—the accidental, the special, the individual, the particular. But nothing is haphazard and self-determined, and it is just the accidental and the unpremeditated which are profoundly significant, for they draw an unknown effect, the consciousness of a whole world of new qualities, whose emergence proves it to be not an accident but a still deeper necessity. Art's accidents are straws which show which way blow the winds of the human soul.

In its view of the importance of the accident and the exception, art shares common ground with science. The difference is, such an accident is to science signal for a new synthesis, for a hypothesis still more all embracing and homogeneous; with art it is the occasion for the discovery of a whole host of new qualities, of a rich and before-unnoticed heterogeneity. With science the interesting and unexpected leads to a new view of outer reality. With art it unlocks new worlds in the heart.

Art cannot in essence be different from other cooperative social processes. A man, out of the materials of reality and his own experience, makes a product not for himself but for others. This may be an art-work or a hat. The action changes him; a man who has made something is not the same as one who has not grappled in this way with the material of reality. This product in turn is exchanged with that of another man who, by the receipt of the product, is also changed. Suppose the product is a house. The architect-builder is different from a savage because he builds, handles material, knows the nature of matter; the housed man is different from the naked savage because he is protected and safe.

The art process is in essence the same. The artist, out of his experience and knowledge of reality, constructs an art-work and exchanges it for his daily bread with a man who, because of his experience of that art-work, is different. It may or may not be that the creation of an art-work is "higher" than the creation of a house, and the enjoyment of an art-work "higher" than the enjoyment of warmth and protection from the ele-elements. That will depend on what scale of values one has at the time. To a starving man no Raphael has a higher value than bread. It is better to say the art-work is more complex, is "richer," or "secondary." Simpler and primary is the building and living in the house, for without the house, the food, or the clothes, the art-work is impossible either to creator or appreciator.

To build the house, the architect or builder uses a technique evolved by other men, a long chain of culture stretching back to pre-history. To live in it, the householder draws on a long evolution of manners, of politeness, of family life, of games and household occupations, of entertainments and conventions. The same social evolution is the basis of the artist's and reader's technique. The whole building and transport trade sustains the architect, the whole printing and bookselling trade the author. The ramifications ultimately penetrate all society, for all society cooperates to feed and sustain and develop the builder and artist and his connexions.

Thus the artistic process is an economic process in the same way as the building, hat-making, or food-growing process. It is secreted in the skin of society. If this seems to vulgarise and cheapen the artistic process, this is because the building and hat-making process has been vulgarised and cheapened, and is now in turn vulgarising and cheapening art. How this is done is the story of the development of bourgeois social relations.

The bourgeois denied the right of any man to exercise dominating power over another. This was because he had long been dominated, and he now revolted. Slave-owning, in which the right to own the services of hat-makers and verse-writers is vested in members of a class, is forbidden by the bourgeois. The only right is the right to own property.

This right reveals itself to be the right to establish a new economy in which social relations are—not severed, that is impossible—but disguised everywhere as a cash nexus. Man produces, not for other men but for a market, for *cash*. His products and his labour power are justified—he can only exist at all, insofar as these bring in cash, and he in turn has no claims on other men except through the market. Goods appear on this market from nowhere, anonymously; all he needs to get them is to produce the cash. Not now merely "pecunia," but every marketable commodity, "non olet."

The law of life for every man becomes therefore to get for his labour power or for his products as much cash as he can, and give as little as possible for other products or for the labour powers of others. He becomes then an individualist. His social task is just this, to get cash, to get the products and labour powers as they mysteriously appear as easily as possible. All the cooperation essential to society is veiled, and each man seems to work for himself *via* the market, in which goods mysteriously appear and disappear according to the "laws of supply and demand."

The result is "commodity-fetishism." The commodity, tangible and ownable, a crystalisation of the social cooperation of man, seems all in all. The house, not the building or living in it, seems the social product. Food, not its preparation or digestion, seems the important thing. Finally, and most fatally to art, the art-work itself, not its fashioning or its appreciation or the experience that led to and results from these, seems to contain all the value of art.

All the time, this freedom, this relation only to things, has really veiled a domination over men. For the bour-

geoisie—now *capitalists*, who own the means of production—dominate those men who have to sell their labour
power to produce goods by working these means of
production. Bourgeoisie and exploited alike are ignorant
of the fact that no one is really free, not even the bourgeoisie; that the laws of supply and demand are not
laws, but accidents of blind anarchy; and that at every
step they are helplessly in the grip of poverty, war, and
superstition precisely because they do not see, behind
commodities, markets, and cash, the social relations of
which these products are only a stage.

But in the springtime of bourgeois revolution, nothing is seen or felt but the rebellion of the "free-man"
against feudal restraints. This revolt was made possible
in England by the alliance of the upstart Tudors with
the upstart bourgeoisie; together they revolted against
the feudal class and crushed them. Around the throne
gathered the new free men, the bourgeoisie, with all
their hopes and desires, their growing sense of power,
their fresh revolutionary curiosity. Of this class,
Shakespeare was the spokesman.

This is still bourgeois *revolution*. The bourgeois market and all it means is not yet fully in being. Shakespeare expresses all the hopes of these confident revolutionaries who believed they had freed man from all
domination, and at last permitted him to be himself.
Shakespeare asserts the individuality of man: the freedom that lies in the overpowering, if need be in the out-
rageous, expression of all that a man, alone in the heart
of him, really and distinctively is. His characters know
only one law—to be the thing they are; and to be the
thing they are is to call into existence, like a magic
lantern projection of the soul on the universe, all the
phantasmagoria of events and forces that is reality and,
revolving around them, is their tragedy or comedy, and

claims them or saves them. That Hamlet, Macbeth, Othello, Lear, Romeo and Juliet, Antony and Cleopatra have to the last verse, to the death, been completely the things they are, without abating one iota to any compulsion of law, Fate, God, or family is just what is the noblest feature of their tragedies and the thing by which even in death they seem to triumph over circumstances. They fail gloriously; they die full of life, for this death inevitably follows from this expression of the Self and is in fact its last supreme epiphany. Yet it is a clear example of Shakespeare's penetration that this great bourgeois poet was a pessimistic poet. He saw clearly that this rich expression of the will led only to death and sterility. This supreme assertion of personal life was always the gloomy road to darkness and not-life. At last he grew tired of this phantasy of the creative personal will which, like a magic wand, could do what it desired. That desire always proved to mean so little. Like Prospero he broke his wand and went into retirement.

Art, in this early bourgeois age, is still quite clearly social process. There is no "market" for plays. The playwright, like the actor, is a royal servant, an officer attached to the visible leader of the ruling class of the state. He is a functional member of society. He does not produce commodities in the form of *art-works*. He participates in a process—the presentation of a play—in which the whole mechanism is clear. Behind in the wings, waiting among the cast, is the anxious author, and there, visibly, on the stage, is the art process taking place; while in front, in the amphitheatre, the appreciation is simultaneously proceeding, and here, being transformed by the art process, are those members of the ruling revolutionary class whose triumphant insurgence these plays express.

The absolutist Tudors are only a phase of the bourgeois revolution, just as the dictatorship of the proletariat is only a phase of the proletarian revolution. The full bourgeois state comes later into being as a democratic constitutional state. The bourgeois has then achieved his desire, which is that there should be no overt dominating relations over men because these would involve dominating relations over himself. There are to be only dominating rights over property, and these veil domination by the bourgeoisie over an exploited class. These rights, inaugurated by Tudorism in a revolutionary way as the dictatorship of the bourgeoisie, are now to be established as the democracy of the bourgeoisie, that is, are to be accepted as part of the given order of things. When categories are first imposed, they seem arbitrary, violent, the expression of individual personalities. This is the keynote, therefore, of the Elizabethan age—arbitrariness, violence, and individualism. When one is born into these categories, so that from childhood one's mind is moulded by them, they seem reasonable, peaceful, and impersonal. This transition therefore from bourgeois social relations violently imposed by the arbitrary will of the Tudors, and *nouveaux riches* courtiers, from above, to the elimination of these wills and the acceptance of these relations as something eternal and just and necessary outside all human will, is the transition from Elizabethanism to the 18th century. This task, which is the completion of a revolution, is pressed on by the smaller bourgeois who supported the bourgeois courtiers in order to secure the death of feudalism, but were by no means content to be dominated by their wills and their monopolies. They demanded a fair field, a free market, and no royal favour.

The effect on the artist of this logical outcome of the bourgeois revolution is profound. If we call the Civil War the second part of the bourgeois revolution, we can distinguish three stages with their stylistic expressions—the post-Elizabethan but pre-revolutionary period (Webster, Tourneur, Donne, Crashaw, Herbert, Vaughan, and the other metaphysicists); the revolutionary period itself (Milton and Marvell); the post-revolutionary consolidation (Dryden, the Restoration playwrights, and Defoe).

Webster and Tourneur express the nemesis of Elizabethan individualism, the decay of the arbitrary individual will that had established bourgeois rights. It is no longer a force making for growth, luxuriance, and freedom; it is a force making for corruption, for evil, for a kind of lax degeneracy, the peculiarly mean, sensuous, and reptilian degeneracy of Jacobeanism. It was already foreshadowed in *King Lear*. The supreme will of Court and Courtiers, once the source of health, is now the source of infection. The Court drama dies with Webster and Tourneur.

Inevitable though it was, this development had grave consequences for literature. Art as social process ceased to be overt as literature. Poet and audience were separated. This separation was assisted by the development of printing, or, rather, the growth and prestige of printing derived its cause from the extinction of overt social organisation. Each bourgeois was to live for himself, connected only by the market. Between stretched the unplumbed, salt, estranging sea.

Art in Donne and the metaphysicals now "withdraws from Court," from the corruption of the arbitrary dominating individual will, and becomes bourgeois and republican. To these men the movement appears symbolically as a kind of self-imposed exile, as a retraction of the garment's hem from the Court and its glittering corrupt life. The battle reaches a bloody issue in the soul of Donne. All his sensual vigour, all his carnal delight in the pageant of life, all his intellectual richness, are powerfully drawn to the Court and to everything he sees as magnificent in the life of the flesh and the individual will. But equally all that makes him a child of his time, all that he feels of resentment as a petty bourgeois put upon by his social superiors but intellectual inferiors, all that he must suffer from patrons and fathers-in-law, makes him draw back from this brilliant degeneracy and enables him to see only too clearly its doom and decay. There are as yet no overt revolutionary forces with which he can ally himself, and hope; he can only despair and withdraw into himself, repent and be at once fascinated by and repelled from the only certain escape—death. Young Donne the lover, gifted taster of fleshly life, wringing from it an acute intellectual savour, becomes Dr. Donne the sombre, eloquent preacher, the organ voice of doom and resignation, Dean of St. Paul's. Born with the possibilities of being a great Elizabethan or a dignified Augustan, Donne was by his age forced into the mould of a tortured metaphysical. None knew better than he the foresworn fascination of the Court, and he endeavoured in compensation to make even death a magnificent intrigue.

All the writers of this age reflect the same process—withdrawal from the Court and from the arbitrary degenerate will, into oneself. With Herbert and Vaughan and Cowley it is puritanism; with Herrick it is pastoral; with Crashaw it is Catholicism; with Jeremy Taylor and Thomas Browne it is a sombre magniloquent Christianity. This retreat into oneself and into the ideal world of religion is also a retreat from worldliness and the sensuous material life of the Court. Poetry and language, therefore, which before were colourful, sensuous, and formal, become intellectual, atmospheric, and complex. The Elizabethan "conceit," a pretty glittering courtly toy which could be thrown off in conversation, becomes the highly intellectual wire-drawing of metaphysical poetry, hammered out in the study. All the writers of this era can be pictured as away from the Court in their libraries, proud, retired, and sombre, writing in isolation, or sheltered in universities, or alone in country parsonages. The Muse has left the Court and now goes wherever thoughtful men, abstracting themselves from a decaying society, pursue the tenor of their selves in thunderclouds of righteousness and depression.

This is not, however, so much a reaction as the final development of what was already latent in Elizabethanism. Shakespeare had before he died become Prospero, the wise scholar banished from the Court, tired of the collective magic of the stage and the easy public building of phantasmagoria to amuse the Court. Prospero's experience had shown that courts were nests of evil and usurpation. Simply because Elizabethanism decreed the fulfillment of individualism, one will was bound to cancel another. The wills of the bourgeoisie, more and more coming into conflict with the arbitrary monarchical will they had supported only in order to shatter feudalism, were bound to fly apart, to revolt against the arbitrary will, and, leaving and impoverishing the Court, fly to solitude to develop the freedom they demanded because the monopolies and arbitrary taxes of monarchy must be challenged by the traders they stifle. Metaphysical English literature derives from Elizabethan with hardly a break. Wyatt's sugared songs develop without a jump into Donne's pokers twisted "into true-love knots," and Shakespeare straddles the period. The real break comes with the Revolution.

This break is necessarily as important to English literature as it was to English history and economics. When it is accomplished, not only has England become bourgeois, but the English language has become thoroughly bourgeois. Those rich involved periods, which are built up by metaphor, analogy, and learned reference into a harangue, like that of a lord or preacher or schoolmaster *ex cathedra* lecturing a respectfully silent audience, must now become current and marketable. They must no longer obey the fantasies of their writer's imaginations, but they must conform to norms conceived of as existing outside oneself, which are reasonable and are not therefore (although outside oneself) *imposed*. On the contrary, these norms have grown to seem the only possible categories of language. Language itself seems to *contain* them. All writers after the Augustan age and until the romantic revolution seem to be writing with a quite clear idea in their minds of some perfectly correct standard, not an expression of their individualities or of one superior will or exemplar, but something to which they must conform because it is the only one rationally possible. This standard is the autocratically imposed system of bourgeois social relations, now by revolution no longer apparently dependent upon an arbitrary will, but hypostatised as something self-existent and self-justifying. This is the "reasonable" art, the "classic" ideal of the 18th century.

The consolidation of the revolution from Milton to Pope, was also to many a betrayal of the revolution. It is necessary to understand this to understand the suppressed forces whose growth afterwards generated the Romantic revolution. The petty bourgeois Puritan, in alliance with the big bourgeois new man, had overthrown the arbitrary will of the Stuart and secured the body of laws safeguarding bourgeois property as an overriding natural right. But as a result of the chances and changes of the revolution, the means of production of England (still represented mainly by land) was in the hands of a few. This domination, although it was bourgeois and exercised through property and not through men, was still so direct and concentrated that it seemed after all not so different from feudal domination and Stuart absolutism. It was not at all what the Puritan had fought and died for.

The Puritan, heir of Donne and Herbert, had fought and died for complete liberty and freedom of conscience; for petty bourgeois freedom from monopoly. This was expressed most clearly by Milton, the measure of whose revolt, just because it is classic and bourgeois, is not today always perceived. Even if we put aside Milton's life, with its revolutionary activities, because it is literature with which we are concerned, always in his maturity his literary theme is drawn from the revolution in which he participated. His verse was in form more revolutionary than Shakespeare's. Shakespeare's verse developed by a quick but continuous transition, from Marlowe's verse. Milton moves from "Lycidas" to *Paradise Lost* in one leap. There is no precedent for Miltonic blank verse. It is entirely different from Elizabethan, and has no affinity with the tortuous poetry of the metaphysicals. It is latinist, sonorous, full of studied inversions. This does not seem to us revolutionary; but then we forget against what he was revolting—against the easy fluent glitter of the Court, the sweetness and corrupt simplicity of a Suckling or a Lovelace who were courtiers still living in the world of Elizabethan absolutism from which the courtly lyric sprang. Graveness, austerity, dignity, and Latinity are now revolutionary, and to be Roman and classical is to be republican and a contemner of new-fangled luxury. To be noble in style is then to be petty bourgeois.

Milton's theme is even more revolutionary than his style. *Paradise Lost* matured in his mind first as a simple petty bourgeois idyll, the "natural man" of Rousseau, born free but everywhere in chains. Adam and Eve, before they fell, were just such ideal bourgeois, free in themselves, untouched by social restraints. Milton's most careful art goes to describe their easy existence in primal innocence. The Fall, that "original sin" which is the petty bourgeois nightmare as late as Victorianism, is the symbol and explanation of the bourgeois's discovery that even the "free man" sins, that some social restraints, against all logic, are necessary. They are only necessary because the first man sinned, and therefore once he is saved by a revolution they are no longer necessary. So the petty bourgeois explained the world to his own satisfaction.

To describe the Fall, Milton had also to describe Satan, and Satan's necessary attitude of enmity towards the authorities turned Milton's mind to the source of this attitude. He found it in an apocryphal tradition of a Revolt of the Angels and a Civil War in Heaven. This had only to enter his mind to fascinate him, and it is well known that in Milton's epic the Revolt runs away artistically with the Fall. One does not have to be a Marxist to see in Milton's God the foolish, arbitrary Stuart and in Satan the noble and reasonable bourgeois revolutionary. Not of course that Milton *consciously* symbolised Charles I in the Supreme Deity, but his affective associations were such that, try as he would, he could not associate with arbitrary authority anything but Stuart qualities, however nobly expressed. Similarly, in putting himself in the place of a *rebel* angel, it was as something noble, defiant, and unawed that Milton necessarily conceived the part. Satan's feelings while a good angel are an excellent poetic transcription of what the revolting Puritan must have felt. Thus, almost in spite of himself, Milton drew in Satan the type of the unsuccessful revolutionary, large and memorable.

The unsuccessful revolutionary—this was the ultimate tragedy of the petty bourgeois *coup d'état*. In some strange way the unfettered free wills of the revolutionary bourgeoisie begat, not perfect freedom, but blind anarchy and gusty waves of tyranny from the saved "saints." Once more the autocratic will from above had to step in, and Cromwell ruled until the big bourgeois betrayed their petty helpers, and the reign of Constitutionalism began.

Milton is always obsessed by this experience. In *Paradise Regained* he is still the revolutionary, but now he has given up hopes of an earthly solution; it is in spiritual and defeatist terms that he now visualises his revolutionary victory. Milton, projected as Christ, is offered all the glittering show and arbitrary power of the Stuart Court, and he rejects it in poetry as in life in favour of "spiritual things," that is, in favor of petty bourgeois freedom. He will not be rewarded for it in this world but only in the next.

Angels will respect him, not man. In *Paradise Regained* Milton describes in eloquent terms the sacrifice he made when he turned his back on the noble world for whom he wrote *Comus* and allied himself with the party of righteousness, the petty bourgeois party, defeated in this world but not in the next. To be religious and to win in the next world is always the consolation of a defeated party or an oppressed class.

Such resignation, in a revolutionary such as Milton, cannot last forever. *Samson Agonistes*, a character in which Milton is still more clearly self-portrayed as a broken revolutionary, pulls down the pillars on the insolent Court that mocks him. It is perhaps "only a wish fulfilment," but the austerity and naked latinity of the versification, disdaining the faintest tincture of self-pity, give this sad play a spare nobility.

The body of Milton's verse expresses the disappointed hopes of the petty bourgeois revolutionary of that time. Though disappointed, the party is not crushed, even as Milton was not crushed. The verse, sad, sonorous, full of senatorial dignity, does not completely reject the world of sense or passion and is not therefore defeatist. It is patient and resigned. It tries to seize these graces in their free uncorrupted essence and to make them strong and manly. Though an unmanly bickering and crabbed dislike seem to linger on the edge, they are not in the stuff. The stuff is sad and yet self-confident poetry; and it is right to be self-confident, for in the coming years the petty bourgeois will again be the active creating class, the steam in the engine of civilisation. Still later Milton, in the persons of Manchester mill-owners and Lloyd George, will be revenged on the Augustan big bourgeoisie as the petty bourgeois in turn becomes "big" or perishes and then ceases to play a creative role amid the final decay of bourgeois culture.

Marvell often expresses the spirit of Adam and Eve pastoral ("The Nymph Complaining for the Death of her Fawn," "The Garden," "Bermudas," etc.) and also an almost Elizabethan insurgence and individuality ("To His Coy Mistress"). The Horatian Ode to Cromwell is in the republican-austere manner. Marvell is a limited but very considerable poet, and his diction expresses clearly the transition from the metaphysical to the Augustans. For he was never, like Milton, entirely committed to the revolutionary causes.

Dryden marks the end of the revolution and the beginning of the transition. His religious and political coat-turning can be condemned only by those who suppose it was in his era easy to see which was the right God and party to serve. In fact the losing petty bourgeois and victorious great bourgeois forces were very nicely balanced. Puritanism, it is true, was the logical bourgeois faith, with its revolt against authority and its expression of the absolute unfettered right of every individual in the form of the freedom of every mass of capital, however small.

But masses of capital above a certain size start to play a qualitatively different role, and it was inevitable that this development should be expressed in that era by a demand for a privileged class and a weighted nobility.

An attempt to put in practice the petty bourgeois ideal of unfettered bourgeois freedom had led to anarchy. Was not the great bourgeois compromise of the Restoration preferable? This compromise hypostatised the norms of bourgeois social relations, yet it maintained authority, not as an arbitrary will but as a monarch who would in fact conserve the privileges of the class of large masses of capital of the big bourgeoisie. Such a compromise was bound to be successful as long as the big bourgeoisie played the rules of the game, and gave way when necessary to simmering petty bourgeois resentment. Dryden, like all other sensible men of the time, accepts this compromise, and the norms of bourgeois conduct become reason and gentlemanliness, and generate in all its bourgeois complacency and aristocrat-led fashionableness, "the 18th century atmosphere." It is the atmosphere of a privileged class, whose

= 51 =

privilege emanates not from a despotic will, but from established norms, and is kept in check by the pressure of former petty bourgeois allies.

Very important and characteristic of the Restoration are the comic playwrights and Defoe. As comedy the play of the Restoration has this feature: there are *types* instead of the individualities of Shakespearean comedy (Falstaff and Dogberry give way to Fopling and Witwould). The humorous adventures of these types are contemporary not historic, *mondaine* not vulgar, and depend upon a particular kind of plot, the love intrigue. What has happened to drama, what function is the stage now playing, that comedy takes this form?

In Elizabethan times the play, tragedy or comedy, hypostatised the individual will as the first concrete expression of bourgeois revolt. All that was in a man was to pour out in a magnificent torrent of thought, colour, and passion, as a Marlowe speech issues from a Tamburlaine. Now, by a dialectic movement, we have arrived at the antagonistic expression, in which the relations imposed by an arbitrary will, designed to express and release individual action, has been exteriorised and hypostatised as norms of behaviour. A preoccupation with *exterior* norms of behaviour rather than with the realisation of implicit possibilities *inside* a man necessarily gives rise to a literature of types. Man sees himself as one of a series of possible types or norms in the machinery of society. This Restoration and 18th century typification is of course not peculiar to comedy. It receives an equal expression in the sudden fashion for "characters" (like Overbury's) which are careful descriptions of types like the happy milkmaid or the country gentleman. The essays of Addison and Steele are developments of such type creations, and Dryden's "Absalom and Achitophel," "The Medal" and "Mac

Flecknoe," show Elizabethan individualities in the process of becoming types. This typification may also be
traced in Dr. Johnson, in Pope, in Swift, and of course
in the early novelists, Smollett and Fielding. It should
be carefully noted that Sterne is free of it. Uncle Toby
and Dr. Slop are not types. Sterne is a rebel; he does
not accept the types.

Such normative types necessarily function against a
quite clear background, the bourgeois gentleman as he
really is. It is said that such comedies criticise society,
but this statement results from loose thinking. On the
contrary, these eccentric characters are criticised *by*
society, that is, by a quite clear idea in the minds of
the spectator of what reasonable and fashionable men
and women should be; unless this idea exists in society
at the time as an accepted norm, such comedies cannot be critical of society, for their types cannot be criticised by an idea of what society should be.

Such normative literature is necessarily satirical and
humorous, and that is why successful Restoration and
18th century literature is predominantly ironical, even
in its historians (Gibbon), and never tragic—at the
most, sentimental. The essence of tragedy and its affective medium is pity, and in pity we identify ourselves
with the person pitied. If a man falls and breaks his leg,
we pity him because we activate a perhaps unconscious
trace of the same pain and distress and fear as we
should feel if we broke a leg. But if he happens to
slip on a banana skin and fall and we laugh, it is because we regard the action not subjectively, with sympathy, feeling as the actor feels, but objectively, as the
antics of a piece of matter seen from the outside. It is
this ambivalence that gives the exquisite flavour to
humour, the sense of release, of superiority, of danger-
ous but delightful balancing on an edge. It is in fact a

release from an unpleasant emotion, the unpleasantness of identifying oneself with the victims and feeling their emotions.

A type is necessarily something we view objectively, coldly, and exteriorly. Stock heroes and heroines, perceived as such, cannot move our pity. But comedy characters *must* be types—an unchanging clown, Mickey Mouse, bowler-hatted Charlie Chaplin, eye-browed George Robey, or a Restoration Witwould and Fopling. Hence a culture at a period when its interests are mainly normative will necessarily be mainly interested in the type and predominantly comic; similarly, when interested in the individual, its art will be predominantly tragic. Of course all eras will contain tragedy and comedy, but in a tragic age, comedy will become as individualised as possible, will become almost tragicomic. Are not Falstaff and Don Quixote both tragic-comic figures?

The preoccupation of Restoration comedies with intrigue needs little further explanation. Intrigues are the outcome of elaborate social conventions, regarded as normative and external, and depend on types acting in an expected way—expected to the onlooker.

This period also sees the virtual birth of the bourgeois novel, although Lyly and even earlier writers could in a sense be claimed as its parent. In the important sense, Defoe is the first English novelist. In view of the expansion of the novel in subsequent English literature, we must examine the reason for its birth now and the part it plays in art.

The novel is a connected story. In this it differs from the lyric, which is a purely personal expression like the essay. Does this mean the novel is objective and the poem subjective? No, this is simply to play about with

= 54 =

philosophical opposites like metaphysicians, without getting inside their skins.

A poem is subjective in that it expresses quite simply a mood, reaction, opinion, or impression of the author. It is meant to be read; the reader has to put himself quite in the poet's place, feel for the moment as he feels, see with his eyes. This is a process of identification. In order for this to be possible, the poem must be objective, must be completely cast off like a snake's skin from the poet's personal mind and completely present in the social world of language so that, entering into that social world, the reader can creep completely inside the skin he finds there. There must not be a tenant already there.

By contrast, a novel is objective in that it presents a mimic scene in which the reader enters as spectator not sufferer, surveying this character and that, this, or that action, as they are borne past him on the stream of time, and never identifying himself with one consciousness in which everything floats suspensively as in a poem. In this sense a novel is like sculpture, three dimensional. You can walk around it. It is objective.

But in order to become objective in this sense, the whole story, characters and scenes, must be quite clearly demarcated in the writer's mind, without ambiguity. A poem is fuzzy, and its values and meanings flow into the real world in all kinds of unexpected rivulets. A novel is self-determined and self-driving. All its world, all its motives and characters and actions, are contained within itself, within its covers. It is a solid, little world, but it is by itself. The poem is a fluid, informous, phantom piece of a world, but it is a piece of the real world of experience. The solid little world of the novel is not real or historical; it is created within the author's mind. It is then subjective.

The fact that both novels and poems are at once both subjective and objective must be clearly understood if we are to comprehend their more recent developments. Of course the bourgeois, brought up on a diet of dualism, cannot conceive that subject and object are not mutually exclusive opposites. In fact complete objectivity brings us back to complete subjectivity and vice versa. Wittgenstein's "refutation" of solipsism (*Tractatus Logico-Philosophicus*)[1] is to the point. If the whole world is only my phenomena, as the solipsist asserts, then it is objective, for the ego is not given in "my" phenomena, any more than the eye is given in the field of vision. To vision, only the visual field exists. To the mind, only the perceptual field, i.e., the objective world, exists. Hegel in the same way "refutes" mechanical materialism. It is, he says, *idealism*. All phenomena are, to mechanical materialism, movements of matter. What is matter? It has hardness, solidity, size—qualities—but all these are concepts, universals, or *Ideas*. All phenomena therefore are made of ideas. In other words, as long as we suppose subject and object are self-determined, forgetting that the subject, as part of reality, is tied to the object, and vice versa, we get these contradictions, and with them the pointless dualisms that make use of "subjective" and "objective" as literary criteria, both misleading and time-wasting.

With Defoe the novel is objective in the sense we have explained: a mock world is created, completely articulated, and held within the author's mind. This world, which is like a self-contained, walled-in peepshow with only a small hole in one wall to which the reader applies his eye, is projected into the social world of language and lies there, a separate object, for any

[1] *Tractatus Logico-Philosophicus* (London: Kegan Paul, Trench, Trubner, 1922), 5.621-5.64.

= 56 =

reader to put his eye to. *Robinson Crusoe, Moll Flanders, Joseph Andrews,* and *Humphrey Clinker* are each such self-contained peepshows.

All such worlds, however real they seem, are therefore worlds of fantasy. That is why the same technique as produced *Robinson Crusoe* or *Moll Flanders* could give rise to a *Gulliver's Travels, Rasselas, Candide,* and *Peter Wilkins.* For if you insulate your peepshow world, and make it completely objective and self-determined, it becomes a law to itself and therefore subjective. Thus Robinson Crusoe is in a sense realistic, and in another sense fantastic, a Wellsian Romance.

To the bourgeois, however, subject and object are always irreconcilable opposites. He is always aiming artistically at the closed world of physics, independent of the observer, which he can watch from outside, and understand impersonally like a machine. This search for a closed world of story, reflecting society and yet completely self-determined, and the impossibility of ever succeeding in this search because it is self-contradictory, is really the history of the bourgeois novel. At first the closed world is unconscious, arising naturally from current narrative technique, such as that of Defoe's. Later it is conscious, giving rise to a highly artificial, carefully-thought-out technique, such as that of James. It is parallel to precisely the same aim set itself by Newtonian physics and, like it, develops into increasing self-contradiction and mentalism. It is an outcome of the bourgeois position, of the bourgeois, as an individual without social restraints or relations, self-determined and completely cognizant of the laws determining his environment, which laws do not, he thinks, determine *his* being.

Robinson Crusoe is a bourgeois epic, as significant in its way as *Paradise Lost.* Like it, it is an unconscious parable of the bourgeois position, as if Defoe had read Marx. Robinson Crusoe on his island, absolutely alone and completely free, yet calls into existence a bourgeois world. Even the exploited proletariat is there in the person of the ignorant, good-natured Man Friday, and as the bourgeois always dreams, there is no overt domination in their relationship—Friday is exploited quite in the best paternal manner. Of course this simplicity of the bourgeois social world is possible only while this art of the novel, which consciously mirrors the adventures of men in social life, is still as young as the culture. The content is simple and appealing; but the form is the parent of all bourgeois novels, for here is the closed world of the novel. Everything outside is excluded by the device of making the author the narrator, so that every chink is stopped up. The island, Crusoe and his thoughts—all these are isolated, eternal, and objective, as absolute as Newton's space and time.

The same device is followed in Moll Flanders, another bourgeois heroine in revolt against restraints, parent of Madame Bovary and Anna Karenina. She exists in herself; the world in its fugitive contacts with her is simply environment. She is hard, free, and isolated. Here too as narrator she closes the narrational world and makes it a peepshow. In both therefore we may say Defoe does not exist, he is completely excluded, and the novel is objective; or we may say with equal truth that the whole action, the whole world, is inside Defoe, that it is subjective and that Defoe is excluded only for the same reason as the eye is excluded from the field of vision and the ego from the field of thought. Which we say is true is in fact immaterial, so long as we recognise, on its first appearance, the nature of this closed bourgeois world of social action, the novel, which is to play such an important part in the development of bourgeois literature. We shall then recognise clearly that this "realism" is so near fantasy that in *Peter Wilkins* or *Gulliver's Travels* it can become fantasy without an effort. This self-contained world is real in itself, not real as a part of a wider reality, as in poetry, where reality is vaguely conceived as a sea or luminous atmosphere, from which the poem only half-detaches itself.

While the norms are being established, satire and typological comedy reign, as in Restoration comedy and *Pilgrim's Progress*. Defoe was not and never could be a typologist or a satirist. He was, by birth and breeding, so thoroughly a child of his time that the norms to him, as to a latter generation, did not need defence or consolidation; they were simply the real world. Defoe is therefore the pioneer of what throughout the eighteenth century will mark the new bourgeois current in literature; the norms now become so accepted that it is possible to create, quite easily, complete little worlds in which these norms act as common ground between author and reader, needing no elaboration. Anyone put in this world immediately finds his place in it, and the interest now starts to move towards the individuals as individuals, and towards their special, not their typical, adventures. As a result typological satire, fierce with Wycherley and Swift, becomes urbane with Addison and Steele, and then virtually disappears. Defoeism conquers. Fielding and Smollett are not such pure bourgeois novelists as Defoe; they are still infected (particularly Smollett) with typological satire; that is why they seem to us so much less modern than Defoe. In Jane Austen what we may call normative realism, or the "doll's house peepshow," reaches its final development. The norms are so ingrained that in the doll's house absolutely real people can have absolutely real adventures. But it is the climax of Defoeism. Romanticism has already arrived with Scott, Beckford and the "Gothic revival."

Sterne deserves a separate consideration, for Sternism is a special development which finds, a century later, its echo in Lamb, and throughout the interim an occasional outlet. Sterne's world is neither typological nor peepshow; it is sentimental, like that of Lamb, Fitzgerald, Beerbohm, and Barrie. One cannot imagine either an Elizabethan or a Greek with that subtle quivering sentimentality which is neither pitiful nor imaginative, but is a kind of conventional realism. If Chinese conventionalism is feudal sentimentalism, Sternism is bourgeois sentimentalism. In both there are now established norms of behaviour so accepted that the satirist's task of establishment is over and it is possible to move among them critically—not with destructive criticism but with appreciative criticism, as of one loving even the flaws and knots in the wood. This appears as an affectionate cherishing of the oddities of "essential" human nature, i.e., of, *bourgeois* human nature. As such it has certain affinities with individual comedy (Falstaff); but the difference lies in the objectivity, the exterior, "Chinese," conventional treatment of the persons, manner, and things played upon.

Sternism then is a slightly later corollary of Defoeism. It is normative, not typological comedy, just as Defoeism is normative, not typological, realism. Its well-bred lightness of touch, its feline acerbity and the narrow range within which it so carefully moves, are marks of an established culture. Of course Sterne is more vigorous and heavier in touch than Lamb, for the norms are less securely established and less historic. Defoe and Sterne are pioneers. Defoe creates the objective peepshow world, from which the author is apparently excluded, and the creation of that world is possible only because of the amount of common furniture in author's and reader's minds. Sterne moves about easily inside this world, and apparently his is a subjective art. But of course in both the important fact is the dichotomy of world and observer. In one the world exists without the observer in it; in the other the observer exists apparently unaffected by the world, coolly and critically touching, handling, and appraising it. Both therefore share a common position—the old bourgeois illusion of detachment, the unconsciousness of one's determining relation to the enviroment.

During the 18th century all seemed reasonable, consolidated, eternal. Gibbon could survey bourgeois Europe and feel sure, thanks to the invention of gunpowder, that nothing could bring about its downfall by barbarians. He was unable to see developing in its midst a tension just as intolerable as that which burst the Roman Empire. Verse, as well as prose, reflects the same uncritical acceptance of bourgeois norms. The current speech; so many things in common that style can be simple and direct; the dignity—easy, complacent, a little vulgar—of the bourgeois gentleman, is reflected in prose and verse.

But ever since 1750 the important second stage of capitalism, factory production, was coming into being. By the end of the 18th century this new bourgeois culture was beginning to express itself nakedly for what it was. How was this expressed in the world of art? By the successful rebellion of the petty bourgeois against grand bourgeois norms and privileges.

Bourgeois culture comes into being as an assertion of individuality concealing, or motivated by, bourgeois property rights, restricted in feudalism. This individuality and these rights, first established by an arbitrary

= 61 =

imposed power, are finally secured as norms guaranteed by the constitution of a coercive state. In both stages the freedom of the individual is being asserted, first against the feudal monopoly of lay and spiritual lords, secondly against autocracy. Bourgeois ideology is therefore permeated with the idea of liberty, of the individual, of self-expression, of freedom of speech and conscience. This ideal serves always as a springboard for revolt against all domination and oppression which affects any one portion of the bourgeois class as the result of the higher development of another part.

Of course bourgeois private property cannot give birth to anything but bourgeois exploitation. There are two stages: in the first, the big bourgeoisie, fat with the seizure of monastic and lay lands, rule the roost; in the second the petty bourgeoisie have their revenge, but produce as a result, for all their ideals, only a still more unfree culture, because their revolt hastens the development of capitalist economy.

The petty bourgeoisie, as we saw in the case of Milton, were betrayed after the Cromwellian revolution. The aristocracy brought back the Stuarts and in the "Glorious Revolution" of 1688 secured their own basis. These huge masses of land capital, derived from sheep-farming and the enclosure of common land, beat the small bourgeois all the time. Resentfully he watched the luxury and success of the Vanderbilts of his day, and meanwhile, having learned that capital alone makes man free in bourgeois civilisation, he did his best to accumulate it by exercising the Puritanical virtues of sobriety and thrift. Thus the two moralities, Church of England laxity and Puritanical sobriety, ran parallel to the qualitative difference between small and large masses of capital in 18th century England. The development of machinery changed the scene. It was now possible for the quite small masses of capital acquired by thrift to show the expansive, vigorous, profit-making powers of larger masses. From 1750 onwards therefore the petty bourgeois begins to become rich until, by the start of the 19th century, there is Liberalism, Free Trade and Cobdenism, and the party of the developing petty bourgeois which, in order to bring down the big bourgeois, invokes the aid of "the people," is inspired by democracy, and pushes on with reform and the development of industry. The Romantic Revolution chronicles the revolt and all the optimistic hopes of the long-crushed petty bourgeois class. This developing class finds itself tied by social restraints, by long recognised social norms, just as was feudalism. In the same way, therefore, it conceived its revolt as a revolt of the individual, the assertion of individuality against the forms of society, the sole rightness of the ego. But the norms against which it revolted were different from feudal norms; hence the second bourgeois revolution is different from the first, in spite of many affinities.

All the period from Marlowe to Milton was the same assertion of the individual against social norms and, therefore, had an immediate fascination for the revolting petty bourgeois. Elizabethan poetry, but above all Shakespeare, supreme expression of this revolution, was rediscovered during this era and found a thrilling echo in the petty bourgeois bosom. The sudden impact of this almost forgotten literature influenced art throughout the succeeding century. Keats and Wordsworth seem to skip the long period of big bourgeois supremacy and return straight to Shakespeare and Milton.

Of course Romanticism was more than a literary fashion. When one has returned to a place, it is not the same as being there, just because of the journey out. The Elizabethans merely asserted individuality. They were revolutionaries striding forward. The Romantics asserted a return to individuality. They were therefore men suffering from original sin; they were *Golden Agers.*

The bourgeois claims the expression of his individuality by the assertion of certain rights. This claim is self-contradictory because ultimately the development of these rights must cripple his individuality. When this crippling takes place, he revolts by asserting still more vehemently his individuality and bourgeois rights, which assertion in turn increases the development of the social forces he hates. Thus the Romantics are mirror-revolutionaries. They attempt to return towards the past (early bourgeois individualism) and in doing so, as if the goal were only mirrored, stride into the future (the development of bourgeois exploitation). This is their tragedy and the pessimism implicit in their situation. The classic world was a similar mirror world to the bourgeois of the Renaissance.

Of course to one who gropes for the past, almost any past is good enough. The rigid hierarchic "Gothic" world seemed, to the unhistoric bourgeois, *anti-contemporary,* and therefore individualistic, grotesque, bizarre, full of sources of free action, magic and mystery. This most unmysterious and terre-à-terre age was given a fictitious bourgeois air which even today it still wears. It was made romantic.

One of the characteristics of this groping for the past was Godwinism or Rousseauism—the fable of an imaginary "natural man," corrupted by the property, religious and marriage laws of 18th century bourgeois culture. This Rousseau-individualism reaches its most eloquent development in Shelley, just as romantic or Gothic-Elizabethan individualism attains its zenith in

= 64 =

Keats. In Wordsworth it appeared as the healing power of nature, and as a return to solitude. In solitude, away from all social restraints and relations, the bourgeois reveals his natural self, his divine childhood, intimator of immortality before it became corrupted by the social norms. It is true that, in this situation, the ruralising bourgeois is sustained by a "small private income" i.e., by the vast elaborate fabric of bourgeois society and the exploitation on which it is based. It is true that he meditates in solitude with a consciousness whose form and elaborate contents have all been given by bourgeois society. It is true that his solitude is a wilderness in fact tempered and cleared of wild beasts by centuries of social labour. But these reflections never occur to the bourgeois. To him it is quite an easy task to throw away society and its obligations and exploitations and be a rural parasite, because social relations have always been veiled by cash. Whatever one has the money to do one can do, for the possession of the money is the sign of one's right to do with it what one will.

Keats, Shelley, and Wordsworth represent three main currents of the petty bourgeois revolution, and their styles reflect the same flow. Keats, richly individual and Elizabethan but occasionally Miltonic, sweeps away the norms and makes phraseology rich, new-old, and sensuous. It is the reproach of grand bourgeois criticism that this is "Cockney" poetry, the poetry of small tradesmen; of course it is, but now the small tradesman, the apothecary and the attorney, are the active developing forces of the age. Shelley, idealist and Golden-Ager, metaphysical therefore, has the abstract verbality and curiously free and fluent use of emotively charged but vague words always characteristic of metaphysics. Wordsworth, lover of solitude and simplicity, is torn between the conversational diction of the contemporary petty bourgeois and the Miltonic diction of the old revolutionary petty bourgeois. His theory demands the former, his artistic conscience the latter. According to his theory, simple, unsocialised diction should be the best, the most expressive, and most individualistic. Actually this "simple" diction, just because it springs most from the individual needs of the moment and least out of enduring social affectivities, is least expressive and least artistic; when using it Wordsworth is least poetic.

These three currents: sensuous Miltonic Romanticism, idealistic metaphysicalism, and nature poetry, are the three sources of subsequent English poetry. (Coleridge occupies a position midway between Shelley and Wordsworth.)

Blake and Scott are also significant. Blake begins by being 18th century, rapidly revolts to Elizabethan Gothicism, moves on to Godwinism, and eventually can find no satisfaction until he reaches a sort of super-Protestantism, a complete individualism of mysticism which is almost psychotic. The most genuine revolutionary, his tragedy is the outcome of an age when, as for Donne, there were no social forces making for the real release of individualism. He was caught in the bourgeois circle. His interest in Milton and Job needs no explanation.

Scott is the novelist of the Gothic Revival. He revolts from the drab norms of bourgeoisdom to describe an age where money is rarely mentioned, where loyalties are still feudal, where all is heroic and the free action of individuals. All these bourgeois daydreams of an uncommercial society were being written, ironically enough, at the same time that Scott was being driven nearly frantic by a typical bourgeois economic crisis due to undue optimism in trading. The question of the relation of observer to world does not, in this historical world, as yet arise, except that it is significant that his heroes and heroines are invariably minor characters. Thus their actions are freer; they are not like the great men who as we can see, even in a bourgeois history, are determined by events as well as determining them. The historical novel, so attractive an escape from bourgeois drabness and the dominating norms, was felt all over Europe to express the spirit and hope of the petty bourgeois revolt.

It is important to remember that Scott is the first money-making novelist, with the exception perhaps of Richardson, who was in any case already in the book-selling trade. This fact will presently have very important effects on literature. Up till then, writing had been done by men "patronised" by the big bourgeoisie, or subscribed by them. Literature thus retained a feudal Elizabethan character. There is not yet the bourgeois concealment of social process. The author does not yet produce a commodity for the impersonal market. He is an honoured servant of the ruling class, like Shakespeare or Homer. But with the revolt of the petty bourgeoisie, literature attempts to "free" itself from the "domination" of patronage and subscription. Its recipe for freedom is the good old bourgeois one—the book is to become a commodity, freely sold in the market. Once again the revolting bourgeois urges on the development of the very things he hates, for the market becomes a worse tyrant than the patron or subscriber. But all this is as yet in the future. Scott is the precursor of Dickens, Thackeray, and Tennyson.

Jane Austen, in the retired bourgeois society of Bath, is the last novelist of the 18th century style. The norms have become so established that freedom to move within them is as limited as is possible for a novelist to endure and live. If Jane Austen's canvas were to contract any more, by a further solidification of the norms, it would vanish. Already it is like an exquisitely bright, sharply focussed, minute magic lantern show.

But in reality no trend is carried to its "logical" conclusion. The dialectic conclusion of Jane Austen is Scott, the big Romantic "bow-wow." At the same time as with Jane Austen in Bath, Defoeism reaches its climax; the novel in Edinburgh, a petty bourgeois stronghold (at that time more so than London), was exploding in the vast dissolving view of Romanticism. Had not Burns already given the revolting Scottish petty bourgeois a characteristic expression, and voiced its characteristic resentment of privilege? "A man's a man for a' that." "The rank is not the guinea stamp." Rank to a petty bourgeois is not a guarantee of value. But the guinea stamp is.

The French Revolution, in which the French bourgeoisie, calling to their aid the proletariat, were nearly overthrown by this proletariat, thoroughly frightened the English petty bourgeoisie. Not only did it cool their revolutionary ardour, making a nullity of Wordsworth in later life, but it also induced the big bourgeoisie to accede to many of their demands in return for their help against "Jacobinism." In any case the petty bourgeois class was rapidly expanding, thanks to the enormous possibilities of exploitation revealed by industrialism; many were on the way to becoming big bourgeois. In England, therefore, the Romantic Revolution now suffers a relapse. The discontent, the assertion of individuality, dies out; there is an atmosphere of complacence. The petty bourgeois class has come into its own by means of the Industrial Revolution, and now it too is conservative.

It will be noticed that so far our revolutionary periods have been poetical periods (Shakespeare, Milton, and

Keats-Shelley-Wordsworth). The novel tends to be conservative and satisfied. This is necessarily so in those stages of bourgeois culture, for the bourgeois revolutionary is asserting his individuality against social norms. The assertion of an individual world-view, of a subjective slice of objective reality, of one's inner world objectivised, is just what poetry by its technique gives. But the novel is the world itself, the whole world of society, in which the individual fares. It is the objective world subjectivised, an objective slice of subjective reality. The writer will not therefore be interested in it if his whole attitude is a negation of current social relations. Nor will he, in bourgeois culture, wish to satirise or criticise it, for this, as we have seen, involves unmentioned implicitly accepted norms which invisibly criticise the mentioned explicit characters. The individualist revolutionary (and this is the measure of his difficulty) has at this stage no norms to substitute for those he is revolting against; he has only his emotional world-view, and this is expressed in poetry, not the novel.

Dickens therefore expresses and delights in the lower section of the petty bourgeoisie, that freed class expanding with expanding industry. There are no real factory workers in his books, of course, but there are the vital lower middle classes and their dependants (tradesmen, servants, potboys, midwives, and so on) and we see again and again the suffering poor—suffering from big-bourgeois exploitation—with whom the petty bourgeois now ally themselves both politically and emotionally. The petty bourgeois class has in fact split. On the one hand we have the Gradgrinds and Scrooges who now play the role of "big bourgeois" shouldering the old-fashioned 18th century aristocratic capitalist off the map, and this class now weighs on the less successful petty bourgeois class on the other hand who, though prosperous enough themselves, cannot help resenting the greater success of others. But the proletarian factory workers are to Dickens, for all his origin, only "Dark People," like the followers of Gordon in *Barnaby Rudge*. So in Dickens we meet for the first time the distinctive "bourgeois pity," one of the most important elements of late bourgeois literature. It is a pity for the exploited as the most suffering class, a pity sometimes used as a weapon against the classes above one, as with Dickens, Wells, Gissing, Bennett, and Shaw, sometimes used as a weapon against the class from which one is rebelling, as with Galsworthy, and finally used, as by Disraeli, as a weapon against the class below one, which has risen and is pushing one off the map. But the line is never distinct. Disraeli is most significant here because he for long alone, even until modern times, sees the proletariat as a quite distinct, *coherent*, suffering class, the Second Nation, and not simply as suffering dregs and sub-men, waifs of industry without class or coherence. He could see them thus because, representing the party of the once all-powerful landed capitalist now menaced by the inflated industrial *petty bourgeois*, he could use the people primarily exploited by these men as a stick to beat them with.

Of course none of these men can see the proletariat as *more* than a suffering class. To see them as not only a revolutionary class but as the only revolutionary class who can succeed, is impossible to the revolting, self-strangled bourgeois artist.

Dickens then is the novelist of developing petty bourgeois society. From this now ascendant class he draws his gusto, his feeling of bustling, busy life; from its false values and illusions he draws his sentimentalities and blindnesses. But there is always life, and a comedy

Elizabethan in tone—individualistic and not typological —for he is revolting against 18th century norms. His people are transforming norms, not making them or accepting them or breaking them. Landed capitalist norms are to become petty bourgeois norms, and all the pressure of material prosperity, assurance, and vigour is reflected in his canvasses, and their own unconsciousness of the nature of the process is matched by his unconscious art.

In this world, Thackeray ministers to the dying 18th century landed capitalist with a faintly critical air, as of one who adjusts funeral elegy to an audience critical of the deceased. His work is polished, anachronistic, somewhat defeatist. Dickens' world is contemporary in tone: all of Thackeray's is 18th century. The class with which he allied himself was being elbowed out of the way by the vulgar, vigorous, vital, petty bourgeois class; and its defeatism is reinforced by the unreality of his technique. The author casts his shadow between reader and mock-world, as if all this was something that had ceased to be, as if only the mind and will of the author were sustaining it. Dickens' work shouldered Thackeray's out of the way, just as his class was pushing away Thackeray's class.

George Eliot is a smaller and yet significant figure. The petty bourgeois was producing its intellectuals too, and in her novels they try to find a way to reconcile the powers they feel in them with the social norms they have transformed. There is in her novels a kind of tension between provincial life, Dickensian and vigorous, and metropolitan culture, Thackerayan and tired. Events are driving on far too fast for a solution to be possible, and George Eliot can really be at home only in provincial life with standards alien to her world view. It is strange to think that she was the translator of Feuerbach, who so strongly influenced Marx.

The Brontës are characteristic of the final phase of bourgeois culture, in which woman revolts against her subjection. Bourgeois development has made possible her emancipation. On the one hand it has produced an economy in which it is no longer necessary for woman to play a non-cognitive domestic role; on the other hand it has drawn up a charter for itself—no domination, equal rights—which woman cannot fail to utilise. But the woman revolts *within* the categories of bourgeois culture. Like the Brontës, like George Sand, she asserts her right and ability to play the role of a man, and to create masculine values. *Wuthering Heights*, the most Brontëesque of the Bell novels, has a wild virility, a kind of quintessence of masculinity as seen by woman, of which Emily's demon lover, Heathcliffe, is the incarnation.

Of course this revolt is bound to fail, because it asserts woman's right to be man, in other words to enslave herself to masculine values. It is like those pseudo-socialisms in which the proletariat is given bourgeois rights. The suffragette movement is another stage. Woman is to be given democracy, and thus she is fooled in just the same way as the proletarian and given the shadow of power without the substance. Later still, in the person of authors such as Virginia Woolf, she asserts her right to build up a feminine culture inside the masculine, as a kind of critical moderating influence. None of these revolutions gain real equality because they are ultimately parasitic on male values. This equality can be achieved only in a culture whose values are contributed jointly by men and women.

With Tennyson and Browning, the Romantic Revolution in poetry spends itself. The sensuous language of

Keats, used with great art, has become a decorative tapestry. Poetry is now something outside life. Its characters live their own existences in the jewelled pseudo-world of the "Lady of Shalott" or "Idylls of the King," and the language consists of words which draw their feeling tone, not from contemporary life or thought or passion, but from a romantic literary tradition, from "old" poetry. Such words have a clear, defined shape like little bits of mosaic; the result is a stiff, colourful, Byzantine picture, quite unrelated to modern life. This mosaic is inadequate to depict contemporary life. Contemporary "allusions" in this hard, glittering mosaic look like waxworks; it is as if one tried to paint men in dress clothes in the Botticelli style, with a result both cynical and embarrassing. Only in "In Memoriam," a poem written originally for private consumption and therefore not fully visualised as a commodity, do contemporary allusions seem less ill at ease; there is a shadow of contemporary thought in it. It is also one of the most melancholy poems in the English language. Its peculiar quality of elegiac despair is quite new to English poetry and is Hellenistic. The poem shows how rapidly the industrial petty bourgeois class has started to decay.

With Browning the Romantic Revolution "explores new avenues" in the same old way. This respectable person, this popular man-about-town, outwardly accepting all the norms of bourgeois convention, is really at heart longing, in the good old way, for the bourgeois springtime that betrayed its own hopes, and yet to the bourgeois seems increasingly more attractive as culture increasingly moves away from its spirit. Early bourgeois Italy and the birth of triumphantly asserted individuality attracts him. Its colours, its enormities, its overmastering self-confidence fascinate him, as they have fascinated no author before or since. Browning is the poet of Machiavellian Italy. Italy comes to him as a paradise of character-in-itself, of character not as a type but as an anti-type, as a pure individual. Browning's favourite form is a dramatic monologue in which the speaker grotesquely or gaudily expresses his real self. Of course this is Elizabethanism, but it is false Elizabethanism, because the Elizabethan age was, in its mode of motion, an outcome of individual autonomy transforming productive relations. That age's magnificent Marlowisms were real because they were the driving power of society. Such a society realised itself in plays in which these characters, giving unbounded issue to their individualities, are sources of energy, and by this mere self-expression produce the revolution of the play—the narrative itself. Browning's characters are only sham; they can dominate only in monologues. They do not drive the engine of society; they backfire. Browning wishes that the free individual, as in the bourgeois dream, was still a source of social progress, but his experience of social relations only too clearly tells him this is not so. Therefore his characters simply revolve on themselves, and never act on each other, as in Elizabethan plays. This is the secret of the failure of all post-Elizabethan blank verse plays written in the Elizabethan manner. They are monologues, not through lack of "stagecraft"—what stagecraft had Marlowe?— but because the individual has ceased to be a moving force of society, in his mere heedless explosion of desire. At the best such an individual can be only a Madame Bovary.

Browning's art therefore is doomed to ineffectiveness. Even though he holds the gorgeous bourgeois past in fee, we get ultimately no more than barren monologues. His attempts on the present are poetically more disastrous. "Mr. Sludge" and "Bishop Blougram's Apology" show how far bourgeois ideology and bourgeois reality, bourgeois hopes and bourgeois facts, have contradicted each other. To be a source of individuality, to be an anti-type, is in bourgeois society to be a verbose hair-splitter.

The failure of this hearty gentleman to escape from the transformed but still bourgeois norms of his age to an Elizabethan past is reflected in the famous Browning style. It is metaphysical in the 19th, not the 17th, century sense. It is an attempt to achieve, by means of elaborate verbal constructions, in which are used abstract terms charged with emotive association, a reconciliation of reality with desire. It is the same method as that of idealist philosophy. It is unfair to call it insincere; on the contrary, it is all too sincere, just as the swindler who cooks his books sincerely wants to show a profit. It is emotional embezzlement; and the style shows all that deliberate complexity, that preoccupation with non-sensual emotive thought, which is always the sign of poetical legerdemain. Just as the fraudulent company promoter covers his trail by a multiplication of cross-investments, affiliations, and paper trading, so Browning befogs his reader and himself to conceal the crumbling basis of his unreal individualism.

Poetry obviously is now seriously ill, which means that bourgeois culture is seriously ill. Three more poets may be regarded as expressive of their age—Arnold, Swinburne and Rossetti. After that poetry is an expression of the final imperialist stage of bourgeois culture, which succeeds that of England's industrial supremacy. Arnold leads a crusade against the Philistine, but he sees there is no hope, and a revolutionary without hope is not a revolutionary. Why is Arnold without hope? Because when he goes to battle against the Philistine, he sees quite clearly his own features reflected in the Philistine face. "There, but for the Grace of God, go I, Matt Arnold." Both are bourgeois. Arnold has his dreams, but they move within the bourgeois round, and when they are given effect in action, they quite inevitably produce Philistines. Sifted through the sieve of action, Arnold's ideals become Philistine realities rooted in the environment of his time. Hence Arnold's melancholy and shrinking from action and his deep consciousness of the resemblance between Roman decay and contemporary bourgeois decay. Of course he is quite unconscious of the *difference*, or the causes; in both cases it seems a mysterious spiritual illness, the nemesis of luxury. Roman slaves and Victorian proletariat would have been somewhat puzzled by the explanation; *they* were not being "demoralised" by luxury.

The fact that Arnold faces and understands the position of contemporary culture, and does not attempt to construct a wish-fulfilment world of mosaic or monologue, is the measure of his genuineness both as a man and as a poet, and of the farther advancement of English bourgeois decay. Because it sees more clearly contemporary reality, Arnold's poetry is able to embrace far more of the colour of contemporary thought. It is really Victorian, whereas Tennyson and Browning are too often only dream-Victorian. Its sensitive colours, its self-distrust, its philosophic eclecticism are all of the period, and give it an attractive flavour. It cannot be great poetry, but it is real poetry. Of these three attitudes which in bourgeois culture can produce poetry—revolution, escape by flight, and defeatism—it follows the third course.

Swinburne follows the second. He is a metaphysical escapist, a follower of Shelley rather than Keats. In the same way he generates a fuzz of abstract, emotively charged words (freedom, light, truth, honour, beauty) instead of using coloured romantic words which draw their sensuous colour from literature and the past and are therefore sharply defined, and do not catch any shade from contemporary reality (rich, gules, spice, musk, revel). These two styles seem to the bourgeois opposed; the coloured, sharply outlined painting of Keats contrasts with the quivering luminosity of Shelley. But in fact it is a typical bourgeois opposition; both are generated by the same thing, and this view of the matter is reinforced by the fact that later poets, like Swinburne and Browning, can write easily in one style or the other. They not only differ from poem to poem, but sometimes one stanza will be Shelleyan diffuse, and the next Keatsean realistic. These bourgeois poets are equally capable of the earlier stage—Wordsworthian Miltonic pseudo-naturalism. This last indeed very powerfully influenced Arnold.

Swinburne accepts very completely the old bourgeois program—liberty (Mazzini and Hugo) and individualism (Elizabethan drama). The French Revolution is now so far behind that his petty bourgeois aspirations can take a political expression. But since reality has moved on, and there is an even greater gap between bourgeois aspirations and bourgeois reality, Swinburne's poetry is even more escapist and swindling than that of his predecessor. It has ceased to live in contemporary life at all. It is simply a metaphysical-emotional parasite upon the past and upon other poets, and this of course is a reflection of Swinburne's own fate in the world of contemporary social relations: the Shelleyan idealistic revolutionary who is also the fogged, sadistic drunkard. The same splitting in personality is revealed in Rossetti, leader of the pre-Raphaelite school. This hearty vulgarian is the leader of an art cult which

= 77 =

has as its motto the revival of realism, the realism of the past. But how can the past by itself be real, for what is real is here-now, is the current system of social relations into which the past has been gathered up and transformed. Pre-Raphaelite realism therefore led back to Keatsism, to the highly coloured, very distinct art world quite separate from contemporary life and built of words drawing all their affective associations from the literature of the past. Meredith, a lesser poet, is partly Shelleyan and partly Keatsian. His involved style has the same causes, and incurs the same criticisms, as Browning's.

The great Romantic Revolution has therefore spent its force. It has led, as it was bound to do, to a profound splitting between current social reality and poetry. They have flown completely apart and necessarily so, because bourgeois reality expressed in current society now completely negates bourgeois aspiration expressed in poetry. It is inevitable, therefore, that the declaration of petty bourgeois aspiration, motivated and negated by the rise of industrial capitalism, should result—for the poetry that expressed it—in the creation of a world of art self-contained, clear, and distinct from contemporary life, and drawing all its affective colour from the past or from vague emotional reflections of bourgeois abstractions (justice, beauty, etc.). Exactly the same negative process, qualitatively different, took place in those grand bourgeois aspirations expressed by Elizabethanism. Here the negation took the form, not of a splitting, but of the complete fettering of poetry, product of Elizabethan individualism, by those social norms based on bourgeois property rights which that individualism had burst forth to secure.

Poetry now takes a new form, and is faced with a new problem. The era of "commodity fetishism" in poetry begins. Industrial capitalism is now entering its last and highest stage, that of imperialism and monopoly, the antithesis of Victorian industrial capitalism based on Cobdenism and free trade. The same currents of thought that produce the difficulties of this stage, "over-production" and "under-consumption," now produce in poetry the commodity-fetishism we shall presently examine.

In the novel, which is not, like poetry, the voice of individual criticism and revolt but of individual acceptance and construction, there has not been the splitting characteristic of poetry's self-contradictory claim. It has so far been free from the crisis. This crisis now overtakes it in a peculiar but inevitable form, in almost the same form as it overtakes physics. The novel of bourgeois imperialism is harassed, like its physics, with the *epistemological* problem.

Before, however, we deal with this last and highest phase of English bourgeois literary art, we will deal with four overlapping novelists and poets who bridge the gap and cause the interpenetration of Victorianism, or industrial capitalism, into imperialism: Meredith, Stevenson, Hardy, and Kipling.

Meredith started out as a representative of the comic spirit. We have seen that the comedies of Dickens, Falstaff, Sterne, and the Restoration dramatists each have their peculiar flavour, emanating from the social relations of their era. So has Meredith's. Meredith is preoccupied with the problem of egoism, of *unconscious* egoism, as it has now quite clearly emerged in bourgeois society. Bourgeois egoism is not slave-owning egoism. It has as its gospel "My will my right," certainly, just like the slave-owning tyrant, but it also has as its counterpoise, "No direct domination over other men." This egoism does not, therefore, like that of a

= 79 =

Procrustes, an Eteocles, or a Dionysius, override that of other men coercively. Such a conception was possible in the glorification of a Tamburlaine or Lear during the individualistic era of bourgeois development, but bourgeois culture soon found that the development of individuality within the frame of bourgeois culture more and more posed the insoluble problem of giving individuality elbow room without infringing other individualities. Bourgeois society becomes therefore the adjustment by norms of private property rights. Thus the bourgeois must fulfil his destiny, i.e., "get his way," by the most insidious means, just as he exploits insidiously, by ownership of things. The manipulation to his purpose of his rights gives bourgeois culture before the rise of imperialism not only its distinctive complex manners, but also its elaborate laws, its sensitive, mock-modest impact on the sensibilities. The bourgeois Englishman has learned Christ's lesson. He has found the maxim "The meek shall inherit the earth" is true, always provided that behind his meekness of manners, he sticks rigidly to his "rights," the rights decreed by bourgeois norms. This is the famous English modesty which, as all foreigners have recognised, conceals a deep and complete egoism.

Meredith therefore treats, just as does Sophocles in *Antigone* and Marlowe in *Tamburlaine*, of egoism, but with him it is necessarily Victorian egoism, that is, egoism getting its way by playing the rules of the game in a sporting way. In *The Egoist* Willoughby is a Procrustes or Nero in nature but he is also a sportsman and a gentleman by training. Created by Marlowe, Sir Willoughby would have violently inflicted marriage on the heroine, who would afterwards have taken an Italianate lover, who would have poisoned him. Three centuries later, a similar situation gives rise to a most intricate and sparkling comedy, in which the characters stalk each other through an elaborate brushwood of rights, manners, and politenesses. Ultimately, Sir Willoughby is fairly beaten by three goals to two. Neither he nor his antagonist fouls.

It is good criticism; but what Meredith fails necessarily to see, being bourgeois himself, is that there is nothing to choose between the villain, Sir Willoughby, and his heroine, the dainty rogue in porcelain. Both want their own ways, and only one can get it; both exploit the selfish rights of bourgeois society. The least egoistic character, the hero, is also the nullest and most unreal character, because character in Meredith's world can exist only as the expression of egoism. The hero is a scholar, for which read "a man out of reality." The scholarship of his beloved's father is of course fine fruity egoism. Thus the only difference between Willoughby and his betrothed is that he wants her, but she does not want him. Both quite definitely are interested only in themselves, and people who are not so interested are like the hero, merely dull, or like Sir Willoughby's hapless relatives, merely the ivy around an egoist. They are never *active* characters.

Not only *The Egoist* but all Meredith's books are about egoists and careerists, and their difficulties in the intricate world of bourgeois rights. This of course accounts for the peculiar coldness and falsity of Meredith's love passages, for egoism chills love and makes it a mere extension of the ego. Meredith tries to build up his love from outside with quite unreal pretty phrases. It is never real and never seems to be a real motive force in his books. They are all stories of the clash of egoisms in the bourgeois world. All his characters, like himself, are *careerists*.

= 81 =

But both the insincerity of his love scenes and the critical attitude of his witty (rather than comic) spirit were reflections of the advanced decay of bourgeois culture. Like Wells and Shaw at a later date, this careerist tailor's grandchild saw the falsity of the values of the stratum into which he had risen. But he could see no other, and so his only resource is mockery, quite different from Falstaff's robustiousness or Restoration typological criticism or even Elian whimsicality. It is like Shaw's mockery, a mockery not only of society but of himself. Just as Shaw's final self-confession of despair is concealed in a smoke-screen of debate, humour, and clowning interposed between reader and characters, so Meredith's famous style gets between reader and world with an elaboration of wit, irrelevant comment, and other superficial ornament. It is the babble of a man unsure of himself, and trying to distract attention from this; it is therefore different from the irony of Thackeray and his similar interposition between reader and world, although fundamentally there is much in common between their temperaments. Thackeray is still in touch with 18th century norms, which support him; Meredith is not.

Stevenson is too minor to be worth much discussion. The escape into a romance now sought rather as an attitude to life than as a world of romance into which to escape is, however, significant. Romance, the escape from bourgeois individualism, becomes an attitude to be deliberately cultivated. We do not create or discover a world of romance outside us, but we must have instead a romantic attitude. This is very important because it is the beginning of the epistemological problem in the imperialistic novel. The same problem shows itself in Stevenson's preoccupation with style, wholly new to the novel but shared by Meredith.

Kipling ushers in the imperialistic age. He is imperialism as it would like to see itself. In this respect Kipling is unique, for no other bourgeois artist of significance was able to be duped by imperialism to the extent of accepting as a view of life the emotional propaganda it hands out in self-justification. It was possible in the case of Kipling because he was a Colonial and moreover an Indian Colonial. Not only is the strict preservation of the shams of imperialism absolutely vital for the control of the British bourgeoisie over India, but also the role of the bourgeois in exploitation is more indirect here. Much of it takes the form of tribute rather than direct capitalist exploitation, so that the Englishman is a feudal parasite rather than an active creator of bourgeois social relations. Such bourgeois as do trade are staff, "sent out" from headquarters like the soldiers, and controlled from England.

Kipling therefore does not represent the imperialism of the big bourgeoisie, who are quite conscious of their role, but the imperialism of their duped servants, the public school boys who are sent out, stuffed full of propaganda and class pride, to do the bourgeois' dirty work and take the knocks. Kipling therefore is the representative not of bourgeois imperialism, which is incapable in its complete cynicism of generating any art at all, but of the Praetorian guard or Cossack regiments of the bourgeoisie. In return for doing the bourgeois' dirty work, they are allowed to regard themselves as members of the ruling class, performing a civilising mission. The D.O. really believes he rules his little square of territory under God and his King, and never suspects that he is the tool of an exploiting class.

The ideology of such a class, like that of a Praetorian guard, will by no means be ignoble, and Kipling is in no sense and in no way an ignoble writer, as Wilde and

= 83 =

Stevenson are ignoble. Such a class will be encouraged to regard material rewards as secondary, for the bourgeoisie of imperialism are not going to have their profits sucked at the source by understrappers. These "Empire builders" therefore are not materially greedy; they may even be ascetic. In this they differ from the conquistadors and East India Company nabobs, who did more of their own exploiting, and kept in their own hands the plunder they extracted from the natives. In imperialism bourgeoisdom abandons the peaceful conservation of bourgeois property rights for the violent inauguration of them in places where they are not. Its mercenary servants engaged in this task must therefore be brave physically and possessed of a real love of violence and force for its own sake. They must cultivate individualistic action, leadership and *morale*, for they will have to operate in a minority, as "civilised" men among the uncivilised. They must be able to endure loneliness and maintain bourgeois ideals while away from bourgeois social relations. To go native is the unforgivable sin, for their historic task is to bring into being bourgeois social relations and not betray them. The public schoolboy in the jungle who dresses for dinner every night is not a joke. He expresses the very important characteristics this class must have if it is to serve the bourgeois efficiently. It is absolutely essential that this class should remain ideologically pure; this means not only a rigid colour bar, but a contemptuous attitude towards native courage, personality, culture, and social relations. This involves the creation of an elaborate bourgeois society for the Empire-building caste, an exaggerated parody of home society. It also requires a constant immersion in European sport or some hobby such as archeology; for if the imperialist's time were not so occupied, he might mix with the exploited native and become infected with unbourgeois social relations. "East is East and West is West and never the twain shall meet"; if they did, they might make common cause against the bourgeois who is exploiting them both. The native class is praised only insofar as it shows unthinking love for its white masters.

Only a member of this society from birth, like Kipling, could express its spirit adequately. Any other writer, brought up in English bourgeois society, would be too well aware of the servile role played by this sham "ruling" class. This class is the mercenary army of the bourgeoisie, and no one has ever doubted that the mercenary is at once a nobler and more tragic figure than his employer, whether that employer be Carthage, Persia, or modern finance capital. Its artistic expression, though limited, may be very powerful. Its asceticism demands courage and its loneliness may generate a high degree of emotional sensibility. This sensibility attaches itself to an extraordinarily varied "imperial scene," of bazaars, and kraals, and limitless tracts of land. It is true of course that this emotion is simple, not complex. Native life does not present many facets to such a sensibility; it is all hard, glittering, quite clear and distinct. There can be no subtlety and ambiguity about it, for the viewer is direct and self-assured. Thus Kipling's style has a bright, highly emotional, visual glitter; but the emotions, when analysed, are found to be very simple. The poetry has the same emotional (not now visual) glitter. There is no "pale cast of thought," but a great variety in the material objects of thought. It is noteworthy that Kipling sees all history as the work of the same class of Empire-builders. They are Normans in the 11th century, and legionnaires in the Roman occupation of Britain.

= 85 =

The ultimate weakness of this art is that, because it is based on the experiences of a duped class, it is unconscious. If it were ever to become conscious, it would see through the deception, and could therefore never become the vehicle of the expression of that class. Thus not only is Kipling incapable of thought, as distinct from an emotional sensibility, but also he is unconscious of social relations. For this reason he can never write a full-length novel (cp. *The Light that Failed*) for this requires a firm grasp of social relations in which to place one's characters.

The one apparent exception, *Kim*, is a world seen by a boy, with all a boy's simplicity of vision and emotional directness. It is a novel without love, problems, or subtleties, and virtually without plot, for the "game" is only an excuse to unroll a long pageant of native scenes and characters, very expertly done. Just because it is a boy's world, and accepts a boy's limitations, *Kim* is his most adult and thoughtful work.

Kipling's successful short stories all work themselves out within the framework of the extremely limited social relations of this class, of semi-isolated men oscillating between a parody of English civilisation and an alien native civilisation. Women play no functional part, and are also objectively described. Love in the established bourgeois sense, with its extraordinarily difficult and complex adjustment of the individual rights of the parties, does not exist. Love is a quite simple relation of the man to his girl at home, or to a mysterious siren, or it is the slave-like devotion of a native girl to her "lord." Kipling is unable to understand the culture of the bourgeois class, of which his class is the unconscious dupe. The English proletariat—even those in the ranks of the army—are quite unknown to him, for his class is not exploiting the English proletariat but the native races.

Imperialism not only called this class, with its loyalties, its sacrifices, and its youthful idealism, into existence, but it as quickly sweeps it away when its role has ended. In some countries (S. Africa, Australia, Canada) bourgeoisdom develops locally to a stage where this mercenary class is supererogatory. It is then quite ruthlessly put on the shelf, or else all the loyalty it has generated is used for brutal war, not against native races but against fellow Germans of the same class. It is of course for this purpose necessary to paint the fellow-Germans in the colour of native races, as sub-human and brutal. The members of this mercenary class are in such a war used as the cadres to stiffen the proletarian and territorial army of fratricidal imperialism. The war propaganda follows imperialising lines, based on theories of sub-humanity and "inferior races." Unfortunately, not only are the Germans not racially inferior, but they are culturally equal, and the mercenary classes almost wipe each other out. Meanwhile the English proletariat itself has been influenced by Kiplingism. For it too has this much in common with the mercenary class of sahibs, D.R.'s, and D.O.'s that sections of it are allowed by the bourgeoisie to suck up some of the profits of exploitation of native races. The proletariat is therefore able for a time to identify itself with the extension of the Empire, for this extension brings it increased wages and increased employment.

This influence ends with the World War. In this war, the world was finally carved up by the imperialist powers, and, in the years that followed, jingoistic imperialism began to die. On the one hand, the mer-

= 87 =

cenary class had had all its morale and sacrifice shattered in the task of fratricidal strife with another mercenary class. At the same time the development of industry inside the exploited countries (inter-imperial tariffs) and the growing contradictions of bourgeois economy had robbed the proletariat of the momentary advantage of unequal imperialist development. Unemployment and slumps set in. It was impossible for imperialism any longer to create art, even from among its chosen tools.

Imperialism therefore began to give way to fascism. This process is in active development now. Fascism creates another mercenary class, the Fascists, but this time it is an ignobler class. It is not now asked, like the Empire builders, to dominate "inferior" races—races at an earlier stage of culture—but it is framed to dominate that very class in its midst which represents socialism and the culture of the future, the proletariat. This task, at once ignoble and reactionary, demands complete unconsciousness and stupidity from its tools. It is therefore incapable of creating any art at all. On the contrary it must destroy all culture. The Empire builders played a constructive part in the development of capitalism; that of the Fascists is purely destructive. This "ruling class," the last and most barbarian Praetorian guard of capitalism, has no art and no thought. Its creed is nationalism, and its vocation is not leadership, like the Empire-builders, but blind following of leadership. Its creeds are built of racial myths, hatred of culture, or anti-Semitism. Against its dark threat the artist, by virtue of the consciousness inevitable to art, must necessarily arm himself.

While all this was happening, the artist who as long as he lived in England could not be deceived by the ideology of capitalism's mercenary class, was wrestling with the problems involved in that more profound motion of culture which had produced both the imperialising bourgeoisie, and its mercenary class. This motion produced was apparently remote and abstract but actually had real and direct effects on literary art.

Hardy seems at first to stand apart from these currents, like a gnarled self-determined British oak. In this he seems a reflection of that English countryside which, like its unchanging grass and daily life, appears to go on and on, while in the busy town man changes and builds and pulls down and passes away.

But both assumptions are an illusion. Even in Hardy's life the most profound changes were affecting the life of this countryside of whose economy he was the spokesman, just as Kipling was the spokesman of the Empire's mercenary class. Old customs, old morals, old methods of agriculture were completely changed. The dialect of yesterday ceased to be; memories and types passed out of being. The gentry and the landowners were transformed or died out; the motor, the wireless, and the cinema came. The changes in the countryside were in fact more far-reaching and important during Hardy's time than those in the town. Hardy, in one of his poems, written at a time of "The Breaking of Nations," reflects on the simple outline of the ploughman who, when all this strife and agony has passed over his head, returns to his ploughing in the same old way. But this is simply not true, for the result of "The Breaking of Nations" is just this: that the simple hoe cultivation becomes the lord's manor worked by serfs and peasants; this, with the advent of the plough and the enclosure of common land, becomes the large bourgeois landowner's property; and this in turn in Russia gives place to the tractor-operated collective farm. Not only is this change in the countryside profound, altering at each stage in conformity with the other developments of British commerce, but it also changes the countryman himself. The serf, the yeoman, and the agricultural labourer each typify different levels of agricultural civilisation.

Hardy, starting from the instinctive bourgeois unconsciousness of the nature of the change in social relations, was bound to develop a particular philosophy when he was faced with the quite undeniable change taking place in his lifetime in his rural surroundings. Hardy feels himself rooted in the country, and he sees this country rapidly changing and dying out. He is absolutely of the country; this fact is the reason for Hardy's strength. Not only does the country in Hardy's youth still retain enough of older norms to give the writer a stable world, with no need for "escape," but also, because a measure of feudal relations survives and the relations of agricultural labourer to employer are not disguised, Hardy has a clear picture of what agricultural society is, although he cannot understand what it is that changes this understood datum. The self-contained economy of the market town area, on which Hardy expatiates several times, can be grasped fairly easily, unlike the nature of developed capitalist production, which needs the erudition and genius of a Marx for its analysis.

Moreover Hardy was a West-countryman; that is to say, he is the child not only of a large self-contained agricultural area—the largest in England untouched by industrialism—but of one in which earlier and smaller systems of agricultural production—the small farm, the work done by a "captain" and his mates—have most survived, so that there is not so vast a dichotomy between landowner and labourer, mediated by agents, as in the North.

Thus Hardy's novels have affinity with earlier novelists such as Dickens and George Eliot, precisely because the rustic economy in which he developed was backward and close to theirs, and it was a homogeneous, self-contained countryside. This fact gives Hardy his rural foundation—his gnarled epithets; his gaunt, simple characters; the reality of his rural background and its inter-relations. His characters really act on each other in a human way (by contrast with Meredith's or Kipling's). They really love (Jude) or hate (Mayor of Casterbridge). This is then the strength of Hardy, his soundness and his richness.

But it is an illusion to suppose the country really lasts unchanged while town relations alter. The town is fed by the country, and sends its products in exchange, and those products are precisely "the very latest" exports of culture: the newest machines, books, rumours, ideas and people. This has, of course, always been the relation of town to country; even in medieval times the country's priests and romances and failings and philosophies were the latest from town. The country has always imagined itself, since the days of the Mesopotamian city-states, as the reservoir of unchanging economy into which explosive modern ideas have erupted from the town, causing all sorts of evils; the description of this age-old process as a modern "problem of the country" has always been the error of the country dwellers of every age.

Just because town economy was in Hardy's time changing with unprecedented rapidity, so was the country. Hardy came in for his full share of these exports. One of these was Victorian doubt: the doubt of Darwin, Arnold, Huxley, and George Eliot. This doubt was essentially a town product. It expressed on the one hand the rapid transformation of bourgeois social relations, generating new physics, new biology, and new ideals, outmoding the old, and on the other hand the lack at that time of any positive culture to replace it except Marxism, which was beyond the vision of a Victorian bourgeois. This new knowledge produced doubt, not conversion; its effect was negative, not positive. This infected Hardy. Doubt gained power over him because the source of this doubt, industrial capitalism, was visibly breaking up the social relations of 18th century bourgeois economy, which bred the faith. Before Hardy's eyes was the material proof of the triumph of new doubt over old faith. Hardy was genuine; he did not escape from reality to a closed world of art, and shut the door after him, like Swinburne. He was a novelist, which meant he was a writer who, at this stage of the novel, was concerned with making an objective picture of contemporary social relations. Therefore he could not ignore or mitigate the fact that all these certainties were dissolving under the impact of outside forces, and that there was, so far as he knew, nothing to take its place.

These developments made him a pessimistic writer, just as Euripides is, but with a pessimism appropriate to that era and that situation. Hardy cannot believe in God or any of the simple formulations of earlier bourgeois culture now dissolved by its own development; yet quite plainly human lives and human hopes are forcibly thwarted "from outside" by forces whose nature and behaviour are quite unknown. Such forces do not play exactly the part of the fate with which slave-owning civilisation symbolised the same impact of unknown "forces," for these were necessarily pictured as the acts of a supreme dominating will, thwarting even the wills of the gods. This conception is not possible to Hardy as a bourgeois; with him these forces

= 92 =

are not fatalistic but ironic. He does not conceive the whole future of man as consciously and irrevocably willed, but it is to him as if there were a spirit of irony in the nature of things which was of itself purely destructive and dissolvent in its action on human plans. Hardy thus clearly and unconsciously symbolises in this form the part played "by accident and chance"— the ignorance of necessity—in the unplanned bourgeois economy. Blind unconscious bourgeois society is the antagonist of *Jude the Obscure* and also the real enemy of the *Dynasts*. Hardy's philosophy is neither profound nor complex, but it is a satisfying symbol, to the bourgeois, of bourgeois life. Hardy, as a rural novelist, would feel most vividly this aspect of it, for it is the country which above all has things done to it and is the passive party in the accidents and mishaps of bourgeois culture.

Hardy's poetry is of a piece with his novels, but the superior importance of diction in poetry makes us note the rugged, uneasy choice of words, springing from the complete unconsciousness of Hardy's attitude to life, the attitude of the passive country to which things happen. It is only such a complete unconsciousness which makes acceptable Hardy's violently awkward way with words, as of one insensible to their affective values and concerned only with their cognitive meanings; but that is not the whole story, for Hardy has an almost Elizabethan fondness for intricate metrical patterns, a legacy perhaps of centuries of glee and part singing in Wessex. Such unconsciousness would result in diffuseness and falsity if it were allied to an optimistic or Golden-Age reaction to bourgeois culture, but springing as it does from a quite unflinching acceptance, allied with a rural passivity and stolid endurance, it causes the verbal gawkiness to be an asset, and give the distinctive Hardy flavour. It is not surprising that Hardy is drawn to poetry, and that the novel is to him an alien form. The novel is the great medium of acceptance of social relations; this acceptance is imposed by its form, inherited from Defoeism. Of course this is not intrinsic: a novel form may be evolved to suit all possible attitudes to life; but Hardy inherited the accepting English tradition and he was not sufficiently conscious artistically to shatter and remould it. Thus he always wears it a little awkwardly. His self-expression is primarily a doubting sceptical attitude and he is forced to include long tracts of non-narrative in which the author directly expresses this attitude. These unassimilated chunks give his novels a starched, old-fashioned air.

After Hardy it is no longer possible to use the traditional English novel form in an important way. Hardy and Kipling were the last, unless we include Galsworthy, who is so inconsiderable an artist beside them. Though, like Hardy, Galsworthy is unconscious of the forces that mould and change human relations, he is, unlike him, also ignorant of the basic human relations themselves. There are no real human beings in Galsworthy's books except Forsytes, that is, bourgeois of a certain kind. By them he stands or falls. Even the anti-Forsytes are, as Lawrence first pointed out, simply inverted Forsytes. But these Forsytes did not in real life exist in the background given them by Galsworthy. His background is therefore unreal and nebulous. His Forsytes belong to an earlier period than that in which he puts them, and, what is more important, the forces which really cause their expansion, tension, and decay are omitted by Galsworthy's saga. In this it compares unfavourably with Thomas Mann's study of a German Forsyte family, *Buddenbrooks*, which is not only placed in the right period, but the forces which bring about its end are clearly shown. Galsworthy's background is wholly opposed to the gnarled solidity of Hardy's or the visual glitter of Kipling's. Galsworthy's London, as compared to Dickens, does not even exist. There is no impact, as in Dickens' characters, between London and Forsytes, none of the pressure and bustle of urban existence shaping urban man. His countryside is worse; it is not in the least real or agricultural, it is a Hampstead garden countryside with apples silver in the moonlight and sunlit haystacks. All the motion in Galsworthy's world, all the forces that rend the compact family of the Forsytes, are presented, according to his own account, as "an intimate incarnation of the disturbance that Beauty effects in the lives of men." Whatever may have brought about the universal decay of the Forsytes, the decay which is so outstanding a feature of the last fifty years, it certainly was not "Beauty." But this remark touches on the source of Galsworthy's art. He is a rebel against Forsytism, but he is a strictly bourgeois rebel, both in life and art. His rebellion takes the form, not of any denial of bourgeois standards of conduct, but of an attribution of considerable importance to "Beauty," that is, to works of art, and to love conceived of as sentimentalised, rural, and unsensual. Love is poetised in passages notably lacking in real poetry. This "aesthetic" rebellion is combined with a sympathy for the oppressed class as the suffering class. This sympathy to the oppressed is an emotion which even a Tory like Disraeli can safely show. It is quite simple, if one wishes to spite one's class, to raise a cheer for the other side, to be pro-Boer or pro-proletariat. But one can do both and remain completely bourgeois and self-deluded, and I think it is true that Galsworthy remains completely Forsyte beneath his aesthetic skin. Galsworthy therefore is compelled to make the forces that disrupt his Forsytes such unlikely engines as the loves of Forsytes for works of art (Bosinney, young Jolyon, and Soames' passion for Irene and for the pictures that cause his death); their love relations conceived of as sentimental and prettyfied (wandering alone in moonlight orchards thinking of each other); and the sufferings of the oppressed (*The Skin Game, Justice*, etc.). These are not really the forces which disrupt the Forsytes; the Forsytes are far too strong for that. They are not disrupted by the loves of the Galsworthys among them for either Beauty or for works of art, but by their own strong desires, by the greed, generated by their culture, which forces them to trample on each other and contradict each other's desires. The Forsytes explode, they are not prised apart; and such an explosion is far more dramatic and interesting than love or art-sickness. It is not their pity for the oppressed that will finally disrupt Forsytism, but the anger of the oppressed themselves (strikes, labour movements, the "uppishness" of the workers). Their refusal to suffer and be oppressed stirs up the whole bourgeois pudding and makes ineffectual both the cruel exploitation of the old Jolyons and the patronising pity of the Galsworthys. But this spirit of revolt in the proletariat is produced by the Forsytes themselves. The Forsytes actively bring about their own doom. Because of this fundamental falsity in his position and the nullity of his own rebellion, Galsworthy is unable to produce living narrative. His Forsytes are excellent, *real* characters. His character studies of Forsytes are *always* good. But their relations are unreal, and his background does not feed his Forsytes, they are merely set in it. For the same reason, his technique has involved no thought, because it is writing without self-examination or perspective. He himself confessed that his method of writing was to sit in front of a blank pad with a blank mind, and it would come. What he has not learned from Turgenev he has learned from James, but he has popularised and coarsened the techniques of the two. The fine point of honour on which they turn—the honour of the author's observing eye—is not there. He has made no innovations, for he has nothing new to contribute artistically; he is too naïve. Yet he is worth this detailed analysis because Galsworthyism represents an important influence in the English novel, and the Forsyte Saga is taken or mistaken on the Continent for an accurate account of the decay of the Victorian middle-class family between 1850 and 1936.

Hardy and Kipling are the last of the major English novelists in the Defoe tradition, that tradition, increasingly subtle and extended, in which the novel is a mock world, an objective mimicry of social reality, which the reader or author surveys as a god, peeping into this mind or that, or turning away to pursue for a time his own reflections but, in any case, quite outside it and unconcerned with it as an actor. Let us call this the Newtonian stage of the novel. This closed world of the novel corresponds to the closed world of Newtonian physics, and is parallel to but different from the closed world of poetry whose final stage we shall presently examined.

Now we come to the epistemological crisis in the novel. The same crisis was currently overtaking bourgeois physics as the result of the Michelson-Morley experiment among others. The crisis was the discovery of the relativity of bourgeois norms, hitherto taken as absolute, whether in art, society, or physics. It was the discovery that the mind of the bourgeois observer, in which these norms of perception or reflection or action were established, was itself determined by the environment on which it imposed these norms. This itself was the result of the general movement of the economic basis of bourgeois society, the uncovering of the contradictions in bourgeois economy, namely that the buyer and producer, whose freely willed desires of demand and supply are supposed in bourgeois economics to determine production in the best possible way and to supply the laws of economics, are themselves in their desires and consciousness determined by the productive forces and social relations of their time.

This is a Marxian formulation of the situation. As it appears to the bourgeois observer, arising out of his discovery of the repeated failure in practice of established "laws," the situation was that everything was proving either tautologous or relative. The laws of supply and demand depend on human desires. Human desires are moulded by society. Society is subject to laws of supply and demand. One simply seems to be treading a pointless round. As a result, economy becomes more and more lawless, uncontrolled, and accidental because the governor, master, and lord of circumstances—the bourgeois—is found in constant proof to be the cog, the slave, the helpless victim of "accident" and the unforeseen. In bourgeois physics a magnificent attempt is made to solve the problem by the principle of relativity, in which the closed world of Newtonian physics is recreated in a subtler form —the four-dimensional. In the novel, various attempts are made to solve the problem. All aim at eliminating the error involved in the god-like observer. Of course this problem, like the relativity problem, had never even occurred as a problem to earlier generations. The major artists associated technically with this change are James, Conrad, Moore, Bennett, James Joyce, Dorothy Richardson, Hemingway, and Virginia Woolf. It is no accident that these also are almost the only modern English novelists, other than Lawrence, who are artistically considerable at all.

It is also not an accident that these authors, who are to be preoccupied with this epistemological problem of the observer, are each in some way alien to the culture they describe. Indeed, to the older school of literary criticism, this would be the cause of the preoccupation of these authors with this problem. But in all ages there have been gifted authors who were aliens, who have not produced the bulk of the significant narrative of their time. Our answer would be that just because at that time the evolution of culture set the problem of the observer as the most fruitful for narrative, any gifted "alien" author would, ipso facto be given a tremendous initial advantage.

James was an American expatriate. Hemingway, during the most important period of his artistic development, was a member of the American colony in Paris. Joyce and Moore are Irish expatriates. Conrad is a Polish expatriate. Bennett is a provincial who, before returning to London, stayed in Paris and became so soaked in French culture that he had absorbed all important French literature before reading a page of most of the important English novelists. He thus saw London always as the excluded observer, as the "Card." The two women are aliens in a subtler sense. Bourgeois culture and art, like that of most older cultures, was and still mainly is man-made. Women therefore who assert themselves, who earn their living, who demand a room with a view,[2] find themselves aliens in a man-made culture. They can, like George Eliot, adopt its values, or they can—a course possible only to a more emancipated womanhood—refuse them, in which case they become aliens, until such time as an economy giving woman complete economic equality generates a joint culture, in which both elements are blended. This sense of alienation is very vividly expressed in their writing by both Dorothy Richardson and Virginia Woolf. Other gifted women writers displaying it are Laura Riding, Marianne Moore, Gertrude Stein, Katherine Mansfield, Edith Sitwell, Stella Benson, and Sylvia Townsend Warner. A gifted woman writer who, like George Eliot, in the main accepts masculine values is Henry Handel Richardson. It is significant that both adopted masculine pen-names. Other women writers adopting men's names and values are George Sand and the Brontës.

I have purposely excluded French literature, but I cannot help noting here that the two most significant names in French literature of the same period, Proust and Gide, are both those of aliens (one a Jew and the other a Huguenot) and that both are writers with whom the epistemological problem dominated their treatment of a theme.

In Henry James' work the epistemological problem is primary; it settles the whole book. Through whose eyes is the "situation" to be seen? To James the alien, late bourgeois culture is not something whose norms are innate and natural, but one whose norms are accepted and artificial. This attitude excludes the "normal" observer viewing the world from outside. James' solution takes various forms, and it is always subtle

[2] Caudwell has confused Forster's *A Room with a View* with Virginia Woolf's feminist essay, *A Room of One's Own*.

= 100 =

and artistic, never mechanical and imposed. The crux of it is this: "The situation must be seen through the eyes of that observer best qualified to notice and bring out its dramtaic and significant elements." This formula, which to James ultimately seems inevitable, excludes the absolute observer of Newtonian physics and earlier bourgeois novels (e.g. Flaubertian realism). The observer is now an actor, and this often involves a shift from one observer to another in a story, but it gives far greater subtlety and complexity. On the other hand, it involves a great deal of what may be called epistemological manipulation. One has first to get into the observer's skin, and then the observer has to get into the skins of the observed characters. This stratagem, imposed on James by his realisation that Victorian bourgeois culture is not something natural but something self-contained and special, into which one must penetrate and whose norms one must adopt —this stratagem rather than any constitutional factor accounts for the increasing elaboration of James' style. The narrative sinks beneath its epistemological outgrowths. The problem is beyond James because he, as observer, is always the "savage," trying to get into the skin of a superior civilisation and, abandoning his own standards. He is not a man with a culture of his own and therefore with a solid basis on which to operate. Nonetheless, James' alien viewpoint gave him a delicate perception of certain important bourgeois forces, and this is well brought out in Spender's analysis of James' work in *The Destructive Element*.

Conrad is faced more directly with the same problem. He is an alien, not only to bourgeois London and Parisian culture like James, but also to non-bourgeois cultures, Malayan, Indian, and Chinese. In theory the sailor, the simple romantic man of action, ought to write simply and vigorously. In fact, Conrad writes with extraordinary complexity, endless qualifications, and puzzling shifts of time. This is inevitable. As a romantic revolutionary, Conrad has abandoned bourgeois culture and sees these and other cultures through alien eyes; but he has no positive position, just as James has not, and his solution, like James', is to make the actor an observer. Thus most of Conrad's stories are pieced together by "Marlow" at second or third hand, and Marlow himself is telling this pieced story to the author.

We have here the same method as that of Einstein in physics. The world of physics is to be "closed" by the complicated method of tensors. The various functions of coordinates, which correspond to the various world-views of observers, are to be sifted for a common invariant element, so that the world emerges absolute, and closed. If the situation between characters A, B, and C is described by A, who is one of the actors, it seems as if we have the absolute world, the closed world "described in its own terms" and therefore independent of the observer. This is the achievement of Einstein and equally of James and Conrad.

No outside criticism is to intrude. The world is described not only in its own terms, but with its own values, as a *spectacle*. "The ethical view of the universe," says Conrad, "involves us at last in so many cruel and absurd contradictions . . . that I have come to suspect that the aim of creation cannot be ethical at all. I would fondly believe that its object is purely spectacular: a spectacle for awe, love, adoration, or hate, if you like, but in this view—and in this view alone—never for despair! Those visions, delicious or poignant, are a moral end in themselves."[3] This rejection of a human view of the universe (which characteristically is considered as necessarily ethical) conceals a complete poverty of internal philosophy and a limitation therefore of possible reactions to reality. Conrad is alien to bourgeoisdom as materially manifested, but he is native to no other culture. As a result, in rejecting its more material manifestations—ethics, utilitarianism, and so forth—he is left with the upper parts of its ideology, its notions of honour, courage, and bourgeois chivalry. These are noble enough in their way, but they are limited tools for tackling the complexities and richness of human society. Hence Conrad as he develops becomes very tortuous and analytical and yet, in the last remove, very simple and unsubtle. His characters, as they grow more and more self-determined, become more and more unreal. His world, as it is closed to criticism and the author, strangely loses its colour and romance. The world, as "a moral end in itself," becomes de-materialised.

We see this in *Nostromo*, the work Conrad valued most highly. The work an author values most highly is rarely his most artistically successful, but is always the most revealing of the author's aim and technique. In *Nostromo* Conrad attempts to create a complete civilisation, a whole town, based economically on the mines, which is self-determined and exists for itself. Yet such a world turns out to be the least colourful and least romantic of all Conrad's worlds. It marks the climax of Conrad's colourlessness. It is just another case of the phenomenon seen in James, Tennyson, Tolstoi, Swinburne, and Arnold: the deterioration of the bourgeois revolutionary. This is a microcosm of

[3] *A Personal Record*, in Uniform Edition (London: Dent, 1923), Ch. v, p. 92.

the deterioration of bourgeois culture. In revolting against that culture and its values, the bourgeois strips himself of all values, because he remains still based on its foundations, whose connexion with the superstructure he has not seen. Nonetheless, James and Conrad have a powerful influence on the technique of the novel at this stage.

Bennett is the last of the realists. He is not like James and Conrad, a fluid romantic observer; his norms are those of the provincial and therefore of an earlier stage of bourgeois culture. In France he comes into contact with the most refined development of the art of this stage, that of French Goncourtian realism and the detached godlike observer. Even at the funeral of his best friend, the author, à la Goncourt, is detached and impersonal, busy recording his "impressions." But in fact, if one once becomes completely "detached," one has no impression at all, for the intensity of perception depends on affective interest. Bennett comes back to England and sees later English culture from a provincial bourgeois standpoint but through the spectacles of a French technique. The French art Bennett was absorbing in France was already old-fashioned in Paris, but being an English provincial himself, Bennett did not notice that he was learning in France a technique which had already become provincial in Paris. Because he has very solid norms and a hard inner core, he is not troubled by the epistemological problem of excluding the observer and making the values and action of the novel self-generating. His values are quite clear and defined, unlike James' and Conrad's, and therefore he can clearly and without epistemological manipulation describe this world. All is hard, objective, clear, full of detail precisely seen. But his norms are obsolete, and consequently his world is unreal, except when it deals with bygone provincialism. It makes modern London fantastic, as if the inhabitants had suddenly adopted provincial standards of a generation ago, and started to think, love, and act according to these standards. To this extent his hard, objective world is quite a fantasy; because it is not intentionally a fantasy, it is to that extent inartistic and unreal.

Moore at first imitates Bennett, and tries to see the world as a detached observer. But he has not Bennett's hard inner core: he is an ex-Catholic Irish landowner and therefore cannot have bourgeois values ingrained. He soon slips out of his Flaubertian skin and with it abandons bourgeois culture. He gives up the attempt to portray current human relations, and this is in itself a revolt like that of James or Hardy. The most important moment in his life, described in *Hail and Farewell!*, is when he revolts against European bourgeois society and allies himself with the local Irish bourgeoisie, who are revolting against English domination, and using a national revival of art as one of their weapons. But although the revolt remains a powerful influence in Moore's life, he does not stand by the Irish revolution but returns to Ebury Street. He isolates himself, stylistically, mentally, and in daily life, from current bourgeois culture. Instead he turns to the past, which is so handled as to provide a criticism of current bourgeois culture. This involves abandoning the novel as a picture of current social relations—a quite legitimate abandonment, for the novel is what one can make of it. It now becomes an escape into a dream world, the method of Keats, Shelley, and romantic poetry generally. The novel becomes poetry. Although Moore was a man profoundly ignorant of poetry and poetic technique, the novel in his hands becomes genuinely poeticised, and the style is completely modified to give the effects of poetry. It is quite a new style in the novel. The transition shows the fallacy of the belief that "the style is the man," that art reflects character and personality as something innate, so that the baby has a given literary style in its soul. By this showing the early Moore should be a different man from the later Moore. But art arises from life, from the interplay between a character and its environment, and this has changed profoundly with Moore in the interim. He had been touched by the Celtic Revival, and its reaction against English bourgeois culture—a revival, however, doomed ultimately to failure because it revolts within the limits of bourgeois thought. It was like so many other colonial nationalistic movements: a movement to safeguard local territory for the local bourgeoisie, who naturally are mainly *petty bourgeoisie*. Such revolutions therefore reach a certain stage and then stop, or there is a reaction because they still keep within the categories of the class they fight. They never really sever themselves from the capitalist culture they are fighting. The Irish revival, which caught up the Frenchified Moore, is a petty bourgeois revival and therefore looks to the past, to a time before bourgeois constraints and vulgarities had developed, just as the early Romantics did. Moore too becomes a Keats among novelists, escaping out of the present into the past. *The Lake* is the transitional work, both in style and theme. It poses on the one hand contemporary pettiness and mean superstition, on the other hand the bourgeois revolutionaries' dream of freedom—freedom from the social restraints of religion and provincial littleness, and the ability to lead a wider artistic and emotional life. This release is symbolised in the novel by the figure of Rose, by old Irish poetry, by life in

New York, and above all by the Lake—an unsatisfactory symbol, betraying Moore's inner awareness that he does not know, he the alien, where precisely to find a refuge from modern meanness. Moore himself escapes into the past, but for his hero to do so, and save himself in his mean parish by writing about the past, would be obviously too unsatisfactory. The Lake, symbol of material beauty, with its changing, profound, amoral loveliness, is what his hero strives for, but actually to gain a fuller life he enters the Lake, crosses it, and passes beyond. Therefore Moore's symbol is unsatisfactory precisely because it is only too apt. The bourgeois revolutionary who revolts against provincialism and the country by going to New York does indeed leave the Lake behind. Like a bourgeois revolutionary, he hastens on the things he hates. In the country he might at least be a Hardy; in New York he will be nothing but a broken down cynical journalist, product of the last and worst stages of bourgeois culture. Moore clearly feels this, and because he does not himself sincerely believe in salvation in America he breaks off his hero's story just as the most vital and interesting part of his life begins.

The gulf between Marvell's America (the remote Bermudas) or Shakespeare's (the still-vex'd Bermoothes), and Moore's (a journalist in New York) is the gulf which has opened between early vigorous bourgeois culture and old tired bourgeois culture.

In Moore's three most considerable books: *The Brook Kerith, Aphrodite in Aulis,* and *Heloise and Abelard,* he is writing with a definite technical aim; he is trying to produce the melodic narrative. This flows on, not by the active relations of characters in a mock-world, but by the counterpoint of the style, by the harmonious overlapping of anecdotes, like a highly sophisticated version of an ancient hagiography. This requires above all a rich prose; it is style, the melody of words, the flow, the course and suspension of verbal melody, and the exquisite orchestration of the emotional tones adhering to the words, that carries the narrative on. The style flows with a Miltonic grace and studied ease, and in its flow the thoughts, actions, and even the dialogue of the characters gleam and vanish, and just because they are always only gleams, significant motions of a hand, a brief interchange of thoughts, they do not submerge the melodic flow of the narrative but are merely variations on a theme, like waves on the bosom of the gliding river of prose.

Such a method can in a novel succeed only with the past, for it creates a closed world of art by virtue of the music of the narrative, in which the characters and their world and their relations do not exist in their own right behind the words, but suck their substance from the words themselves. If Moore were to write thus of modern themes, reality would keep breaking in and spoiling the music, as if one were to try to tell a modern story in blank verse. Imagine the effect: a novel of modern London written in the late Moore style would be the same. To adapt the technique to current events he has to use the "imaginary" dialogues of London or the carefully arranged reminiscences of *Hail and Farewell!* In memoirs the problem of the observer does not arise. In real reminiscences everything is already sited in the observer's viewpoint, is already objective-subjective. The behaviour of the world and the movements of the characters between the times when they impinge on the author's vision can be neglected in reminiscences.

Moore then settled his difficulty by creating a romantic closed world of art, doing for the novel what Tennyson did for poetry. It is possible to create this closed world only by using words and a style whose affective tones will be drawn, not from life, but from literature, and whose associations will therefore exclude the present; this corresponds in the novel to the romantic poetic vocabulary. The narrative itself will be subordinated to this movement of style, so that it will be a masterpiece of prose rather than of narrative; all its anecdotes, characters, and background will not evoke anything more than the author chooses to give, because they are "historical." Needless to say, the characters, though historical, remain bourgeois and individualistic in conception. For example, neither Jesus nor Paul in *The Brook Kerith* think inside a world-view produced by their environment: their minds have no given contents, their actions are those of people without pre-history, rather like Arcadians. Moore's historical world is a pastoral, isolated world, and this is a familiar bourgeois dream. Bourgeois pastoral may be beautiful and charming, and Moore's is both; but its limitations are obvious. The novel's vital meaning to a generation is precisely the view it gives of living, present human social relations. A technique that subordinates the onward pressure of life to a melodic orchestration, and concerns itself deliberately with sterilised scenes from the past, produces a closed world of art that has all the finality of pastoral. There is nothing beyond. It springs from Moore's own helplessness in the face of modern society, in which in his life he had never played a functional part. He had never even played a bourgeois part; he had been a landowner, a survival. This extension of the method of poetry to another field loses the succinct poignancy of poetry which does not have to build up laboriously a consistent world but can at once reside there, and does

= 109 =

not gain the factual strength or rich complex energy of the novel form. Moore had no followers.

Instead we had a Joyce, an expatriated Irish ex-Catholic, alien therefore to English culture and Continental thought. The same transformation of style we saw in Moore takes place in Joyce from the saccharine-sweet *Pomes Penyeach*, to the tough *Work in Progress*; and the change is associated with the emergence of the same problem. Joyce gives up all attempts to view the alien Continental culture in which he establishes himself; he concerns himself instead with his abandoned Dublin life. Because it is abandoned, because it has ceased to be in vital connexion with his latter life and ideals, he can view the life as if it were foreign, as if the old Joyce were simply a clinical picture. Because he has not acquired a new culture or new standards, he cannot criticise this life, he cannot select it and coordinate it so as to establish an affective attitude towards it. Instead everything has to go in, without organisation, selection of incident, or time scale.

Complete artistic disorganisation is in fact impossible, for art is by the very essentials of its technique a selection and organisation. An art-work must begin and end; it cannot go on forever. It must select certain words; they will not accrete of themselves, like a growing thing. All art must have a plan. All mentation has a plan. Psychotherapy has discovered that even the wildest ravings of a lunatic have a simple and logical underlying structure. They are associations to some simple wish or experience.

Joyce, therefore, devoid of a critical foundation in the form of a world-view, is forced to impose on his Dublin life a childish form of organisation—parallelism to the *Odyssey*. Homer's *Odyssey* is followed pedantically and paralleled by "corresponding" characters and incidents in Dublin life. This is a very poor substitute for a plan springing from a stable and profound view of life. It is scholastic and formal art.

A plan implies selection. Selection implies a touchstone for selection which can only be a stable worldview. The world-view implies an observer whose perception is conditioned by what he is and what he springs from. So once more we arrive back at the epistemological problem.

Ulysses hopes to exclude the observer with his definite viewpoint, partly because the bourgeois viewpoint is no longer adequate to the growing complexities of life, partly because Joyce himself has no viewpoint, having abandoned that of the Dublin bourgeois and gained no other. He attempts therefore to create the closed world of art by giving quite simply the whole contents of the minds of the actors.

But how were these contents known? Divinely? No, they were guessed at by the observer, and come therefore from his mind. How were a few out of the innumerable possible selected, and the words selected out of the innumerable in the dictionary to express these selected contexts? By the mind of the observer. How were these contents arranged in a plan, the plan of the novel? By the mind of the observer. We thus find that this method in no way excludes the author; it fills the book with him. Joyce as we saw had no consistent viewpoint; his attitude to reality is fluid, hesitating, and unperceptive. *Ulysses* is therefore hesitating, formless, and unreal. In spite of the gifts of the author, it deliquesces through its immaturity and pedantry, through its lack of experience. In this it simply reflects the decline of bourgeois culture, the

= 111 =

abandonment of its exploded certainties, and as yet no new understanding to take their place.

But at least it brings us to a very clear methodological rule which has been overlooked by all subsequent novelists, which is this. If we divide a novel up into two parts: (*a*) The characters' *thoughts*, analysed, hinted at, or described; (*b*) The characters' *words and actions* described; then all the material in *a* contains *more* of the author, i.e., of the observer, than *b*. Yet the modern novelist appears to suppose that the opposite is the case, that with *a* he is less himself and penetrating more deeply into outer reality than with *b*. But we have gained the outer reality we describe in a novel by *experience*. As regards other people, we *see* their words and actions. From these we infer, as a result of our own experiences, their thoughts and aims. Thus there is a larger element of the "I" of the author in *a* than *b*; there are two layers of subjectivity instead of one. That is why a novel like *Ulysses* seems so little objective, seems full of the distortions of the observer, seems all author and no reality, although it attempts to make its characters objective through their consciousnesses.

The same considerations affect the problem of depicting unconscious motivations. These can never be included in the stream of consciousness, because they are by definition unconscious. They can be detected only by distortions in the consciousness as overtly evidenced in words and actions. Their description therefore properly comes under the heading of *b*. The influence of the unconscious is detected in the disproportion between the character's action, including his emotional expression, and his conscious contents. This is how the psychologist detects it. To suppose the unconscious can be "included" in the stream of consciousness as part of *a* is to invert the meaning of the unconscious.

Virginia Woolf and Dorothy Richardson are not expatriates to the same extent as Joyce. They have more of a world-view and therefore their works are less formless. Their position is substantially this: the woman who becomes culturally conscious becomes an artist and a part of the male economic system—teacher, writer, worker, or intellectual instead of housewife, daughter, or aunt. She then finds herself to an extent an alien in "man's world." This world is a vast cognitive expression of man's notion of reality. As long as it is stable and coherent the woman is forced like Aphra Behn, Angelica Kauffman, George Eliot, the Brontës, or Ethyl Smyth, to adopt completely man's reactions and viewpoint. She may even, like Sappho, adopt man's sexual role or, like George Sand, man's attitude towards love. This need to adapt acts as a kind of brake on woman's artistic achievement, rather similar to the difficulty experienced by one race operating in the culture of another.

But when this culture begins to collapse, woman is able to adopt a critical attitude towards it. This critical attitude is expressed by Dorothy Richardson, Virginia Woolf, and also Katherine Mansfield. Woman's critical attitude cannot be mainly cognitive or "rational" in form, because the cognitive elements in culture, as a result of man's scientific role, are masculine. It must be therefore an uncognitive or emotional criticism. But bourgeois art also is male and is also emotional, so that even here her emotion has to be of a special sort, alien to the emotional formulations of current art, which she regards as slick and artificial (cp. Virginia Woolf's criticism of Bennett and Wells). This primarily emotional attitude must be, for example, quite opposed to that of a Tolstoi; it must be fluid, tremulous, undefined, insecure, and blurred. Those particular emotional attitudes which have not given shape and direction to an art must, owing to their foreignness and lack of ready-made forms, issue as fluid, vague, and tremulous until they have built up a tradition of their own. In the same way these feminine aliens have no historic world-view, because the bourgeois world-view is male. They have only a personal world-view springing from their own experience; they cannot, like men, share completely in the personal experience enshrined in art and culture, for these are experiences of men.

This gives rise to their peculiar art; it is an art of the world as seen by Miriam, coloured with her own values, uninterested in what happens to the actors before or after they swim into her ken, for outside her ken they are coloured with alien values; or it is of the world as seen by Mrs. Dalloway, in which all the affective associations are personal and not historic, and therefore seem to men arbitrary and out of proportion, like Jacob's famous boots. But if I ignore tradition and draw only from my personal experiences, the emotional values I attach to events will be influenced entirely by my experience and may therefore seem out of balance and strained. Notice that although the feminine observer has not, just as Joyce has not, a cultural world-view, she has a personal world-view which transcends personality. It is a world-view which arises from being a woman, from being conscious of a whole series of different emotional values opposed to the contemporary culture, which culture now, because of its evident decay, no longer overawes one, while one knows that millions of other women dumbly share one's emotional consciousness.

These circumstances give rise to the illusion of a set feminine viewpoint and a fixed feminine character, the theory that by nature woman sees things personally, emotionally, irrationally, and with a certain arbitrariness and lack of historical perspective. But this is true only of bourgeois woman; or, more strictly, of woman in a culture (a) made by man, but (b) reaching a transitional stage in which women enter into male economic life and are made free of its culture, (c) which is collapsing.

These three factors, a, b, and c, have been fulfilled by bourgeois culture only in this century, and thus, for the first time, emerge a feminine art and a feminine viewpoint.

In certain savage tribes the economic life and organization is in the hands of women. They wrestle cognitively with nature; they are the progressive active class; and men "mind" the babies and the home. If such a tribe were able to build up an elaborate culture, the cognitive and traditional artistic culture would of course be feminine. It would then be woman whose art and thought would seem historical, intellectual, clear-cut, and impersonal, and man's which would seem untraditional, emotional, vague, and individual.

This is not to deny an essential difference between men and women. Obviously the difference is there, is physiological, and must therefore affect all the activities of the sexes. The mistake is to assert, as essential, the particular mode in which that difference manifests itself at any stage of culture: for example, to regard Virginia Woolf's sensitive, personal, and critical approach as characteristic of woman in the abstract, and not as characteristic of bourgeois intellectual woman functioning as an artist in this particular stage of cultural evolution.

In Communist culture women play an equal role in economic life with men. Sex discrimination in pay, education, and other social activities is eliminated. Woman can then begin to modify cognitive and artistic culture to insert a feminine element. In doing so she is herself changed. At first she operates as an alien faced with and criticising a collapsing culture, like Virginia Woolf. At a later stage she is a constructive force, a revolutionary remoulding a collapsing culture. The ultimate result is the production of a joint culture. At the end of this process, not only is the culture itself transformed, but men and women are no longer the same: man is no longer the uncriticised lord, woman is no longer the critical alien. Of course no bourgeois man is willing to admit that his culture is collapsing or that woman is not, as artist or thinker, innately inferior to man. Bourgeois woman is also arrogant; she is too inclined to believe herself speaking not only for her own time and her own class, but for all women of the past—Neanderthal, Amazon, and Medieval—and not only of the past but of the future too. But in speaking for herself, she has no right to suppose she therefore speaks for them.

Today Hemingway, on the other side, speaks for a bourgeois man who leads a revolt not after all so different from that of women, a revolt against the bourgeois culture which, although he created it, is now imprisoning him and making him emasculate and worthless as a man. But Hemingway is a bourgeois revolutionary and he follows the classic bourgeois party-line: "Back to the Golden Age, back to the simple, natural, uncorrupted man, free from social restraints."

Hemingway's heroes are therefore "uncultured" men, not in the conventional sense, but as men who both in character and as observed by the author are full of the primitive, uncivilised virtues. They are brave, dumb, simple, and full of elementary passion and desire. Because the author is rejecting bourgeois culture, of which he had so intimate an experience in the War, these characters must be described in a way that excludes the traditions of bourgeois culture. All analysis of thought, all pursuit of psychological complexities and subtleties, are full of traditional bourgeois positions, and therefore Hemingway's famous objectivity is designed to exclude the inherited worldview of the bourgeois. It is the old problem of excluding the observer once again, in yet another form.

This has three consequences. (a) It is not possible to describe accurately human impacts because to do so in a bourgeois world requires either deep psychological analysis or an understanding of bourgeois culture. But both are rejected by Hemingway, because they involve writing with the bourgeois world-view. This leads to a world artificially simplified. Only simple types and simple relations can be dealt with. (b) A culture can never be transformed or vitalised by a return to a more primitive level. Outworn hypotheses are destroyed by ones containing greater truth; decaying productive relations are replaced by more fertile cultures. The moving forces of a civilisation are those that are moving it forward. These forces are today no longer bourgeois; they are wielded by the class-conscious revolutionary, who is to transform this culture by destroying and rebuilding it. But Hemingway's characters are not awakened and revolting proletarians; they are primitive men. They are not men who have shaken off, but men who have escaped, bourgeois consciousness. Such men are not active forces but passive objects. Their role is to suffer with ox-like patience and occasional violent individual outbursts all that bourgeois culture inflicts upon them. They are the proletariat seen, not as the creative and revolting class, but as the unconscious and suffering one. This is simply the old familiar mistake of the revolting bourgeois individualist, of the man who revolts against bourgeois culture within its limits, who therefore simply drives on its development. (c) Man, stripped of bourgeois culture and bourgeois social relations, becomes primitive man, *man without women*. All the complexities and delicate qualifications which transform simple desire for sexual congress into love—primitive, feudal, or bourgeois love—are embodied in the traditions of a culture. Love relations are mediated by such a culture. If, therefore, this culture is rejected, the bridge between man and woman is cut. Relations can take place only at the simplest possible level. Women become unreal shells, simple foci of sexual desire. Love is a very simple and therefore unreal passion in Hemingway's novels.

This brings our analysis of the important trends in the bourgeois English novel to an end. The next phase implies revolution and a negation of bourgeois culture, not as a mere negation but with a positive world-view, that of proletarian or Marxist culture. This phase, with Gide, Dos Passos, André Malraux, and Barbusse in Europe, and the post-revolution Russian novelists in Russia, has already begun, but is still far too new for comment. It had certain precursors, of whom the most important is Lawrence, whom I have discussed elsewhere.[4] We may analyse briefly the difference thus:

The bourgeois is unconscious of the determining character of social relations. He therefore believes it

[4] See "D. H. Lawrence: A Study of the Bourgeois Artist," in *Studies in a Dying Culture.*

possible to construct a closed, absolute world of art from which the observer is excluded, a world of absolute values existing in themselves, not a world of values for the observer. The more this objectivity is consciously sought, the more subjective the novel becomes.

The solution is Marxist. The closed world of art is not possible. The observer is himself and in his values determined by his social relations. Nonetheless, the observer can be freed. This freedom is also the aim of the bourgeois closed world of art, an aim which failed only because of bourgeois ignorance concerning the nature of freedom. Freedom is obtained, not by the elimination of the observer or by suppressing his role, but by recognising it, by understanding of the determining power of social relations. The world of art is then not closed; it is open in the sense that it includes the observer, because its social relations in all their determinism are overt. This of itself makes it objective, because on the one hand there is a definite world-view, and, on the other hand, the sources of this world-view are not concealed but recognised. This fact does not lead to rigidity and stagnation, for this world-view recognises the relativity of all values and the change of all being. It asserts that the very ingression of novelty, which is the stuff of art, is perpetual, and refuses to recognise any form, tradition, dream, hope, moral, aim, illusion, or truth as permanent. This, then, is the proletarian novel which it is the task of the novelist to create. This is what has been set by Russian novelists as their conscious aim: *socialist realism*.

. . . . .

MEANWHILE what has become of poetry? Poetry has become a commodity. This commodity fetishism is enunciated in the slogan of the *fin de siècle* poets and

= 119 =

poetisers, Wilde, Pater, and the rest: "Art for art's sake."

But, it will be retorted, surely this slogan is the very denial of the bourgeois view of art as a commodity. The Victorian bourgeois, to whom art is simply a commercial activity like making boots, is challenged by the *fin de siècle* aesthete with the demand "art for art's sake," art, subordinated to no rules of morals, economics, or expediency but only to its own rules. We have seen before that the bourgeois revolutionary in his revolution simply asserts the inalienable rights of the bourgeois; and this is an example. "Art for art's sake" establishes the closed world of art, drawing its values from itself, independent of the observer, whose mind and values are determined by society. Such a world is self-contradictory, and the attempt to establish it drives art in the opposite direction. One gets a world of art more and more drawing its values, not from itself but from the individual, until finally the world of art becomes a completely private world, and therefore ceases to be a world of art, for art is nothing if not social. This is in fact simply the history of poetry during the last half-century.

The romantic revolution in poetry began as an escape into the past (Keats), into nature (Wordsworth), into metaphysics (Shelley). The next stage logically is to pull up the ladder by which one has climbed into this world, and thus cut it off. This is the closed world of poetic art—art for art's sake. Tennyson forms the transition. With Wilde and Pater it is complete.

How is this related to bourgeois economy? As Marx shows, the characteristic psychological attitude produced by this form of production is commodity fetishism. Each producer is unplanned and unfettered in theory; in practice he is controlled by "the market," which is simply an abstraction expressing lack of conscious control. All products, whether labour-power or goods, are commodities in relation to this market. Only marketable commodities have a value. This applies to the labour-power of the labourer or of the scientist, just as strictly as it does to hats, wheat, or boots. The previous history of these products, the story of the leather, soil, fabric, or the nurture and training of labourer or scientist is forgotten. The subsequent fate of the commodities is also no matter for concern. The commodity becomes hypostatised. It seems in itself to be important and desirable and to lead a strange divine life of its own.

In fact the commodity only exists and only has value as part of a social process. This process includes the fashioning of the materials, all the organisation that collected and transported them, and the inherited culture that made them possible. It does not stop there, but passes on to the enjoyment of the commodity—the use made of it, and the role it plays in the life of the user. This process, even in so simple a social product as a hat, involves the cooperation of millions of men, ramifies forward and backward into time, and has its ground in all society. It is the product of, and itself influences, a multitude of desires, skills, actions, aims, and cognitions of men. This process applies equally to a hat or a painting. The precise part the social product plays in determining desires and emotions, throughout its process, settles the respective values we attach to a hat or a painting. We attach more value to a great painting, just because its process is more elaborate, longer-continued, more intimately wrapped up with the evolution of society and its emotions, hopes and thoughts, than a hat. But to the bourgeois there is only one kind of value—market or exchange-value—and it seems to him that this should determine the other value, use-value, which is value accruing to the community because of the role of its process in the life of the community. He feels use-value should be expressed in exchange-value, in cash. He does not at heart believe in the reality or genuineness of the other value. He can only be brought to believe that a modern painting, worth a few guineas, has a really high artistic value by being persuaded that in a century or so it will be worth as much as a Raphael. Of the artistic value of a Raphael he has no doubt because of its high exchange value.

The "aesthetic bourgeois" revolts against this commercial bourgeois reckoning of the art product by its exchange value. He does not see that this reckoning is not a mistake peculiar to the bourgeois evaluation of the art-work, but general to all social processes and characteristic to bourgeois economy. He himself makes the same mistake with everything but art. He reckons hats entirely by their value as commodities. He would have no patience with a crusade, "hat-making for hat-making's sake." Because of this, he reacts to bourgeois criticism in a bourgeois way. To the bourgeois question, "What after all is the exchange-value of the product?" the aesthete replies, "It has none." To his query, "How does art justify itself commercially?" he replies, "It need not; it is justified in itself."

The art-work is therefore justified in itself. Like the picture of Dorian Gray, or Pater's "Mona Lisa" it comes to life, and in itself has all experience and all beauty. Its beauty does not seem to arise, as in reality it does arise, out of its creation and enjoyment, in which process in turn all society's creative functioning is crystallised; but it is held to exist in itself. The art-work thus becomes a commodity, and is worshipped in itself. Its enjoyment, the social role it plays as something appreciated and vitalising men's lives, is thus neglected. It becomes subject to connoisseurship and collectors' mania, the art-work locked away and not enjoyed, as if it could waste its sweetness on the desert air. Art ceases to be a process or an activity and inheres simply in the commodities produced by artists. The puzzling question whether a great painting is more valuable than a little person ignores the vital fact that painting, as art, exists only in persons.

Thus for such bourgeois, once the art-work is produced the art process is finished, just as is the hat process when the hat is ready for the market. That the purchase and wearing of the hat is of vital importance to society ceases to be of significance to the bourgeois. We get therefore "under-consumption." The commodity is produced, but is not used. In other words, art's public shrinks, and it is the fault of the artist as well as the public, or rather both are brought about by the underlying motion of economic relations.

Once the poet sees the art-work existing in itself, then the creation of the art-work and not its social use is all that seems important to him. Consequently the poem becomes personal. The affective associations to words are all personal. "Art for art's sake" is unworkable as a slogan, and really conceals the position "Art for *my* sake." Since the social enjoyment of the product is no longer remembered, there is no pressure to embody one's personal emotions entirely in the social world of enjoyment. The poet becomes anti-traditionalist, and purely personal. Meter, syntax, and other social forms are shed. Words are used for their private associations. Thus the attempt to make the art-work exist in its own right, apart from the social world, objectively and with absolute self-created values—the

= 123 =

aim of the Parnassians and of the *fin de siècle* poets—rapidly results in an art whose values are completely subjective and completely relative, the art of the symbolists, and of the surrealists. Art slides out of the social world, and becomes more and more personal. When poetry has become completely personal and completely non-social, it is then no longer art, nor, since language is social, is it language. It is a kind of indistinct swearing. At the same time poetry's public has shrunk from the same causes, because poetry has more and more ceased to be a social process, and more and more become individualist. Thus the social element in poetry and poetry's public shrink until both cease to exist. This is the limit, closely approached though not actually reached, by many post-war poets.

It must not be supposed, however, that this commodity-fetishism and retirement into an individual world is due to the common obstinacy of all bourgeois poets. It is forced on them by the collapse of bourgeois culture itself, for commodity fetishism and the ignorance of social process are what produce that collapse and with it the dissolution of the bourgeois world-view. The anarchy of bourgeois economy and the disintegration of the bourgeois world-view are aspects of the same process.

The poet depends on a common world-view for the communication of his personal experience. I, as poet, must make over to society my individual experience by means of social language. This implies that I have in common with my communicants a social world, rich with affective values and full of material into which I can project my individual experience. Such a world-view—common, for example, to all Elizabethans—is lacking to collapsing bourgeois culture today. As the total of distinct social world-views increases, as the size of groups sharing beliefs, emotions, goals and views of reality in common decreases, while these groups multiply in number, each poet's audience shrinks. The more intense his experience and the more sharply defined and rich the social world into which he needs to project it, the smaller the group he can communicate it to. Ultimately the social world contracts to a personal one, and the poet vanishes in the phantasist or daydreamer.

It is the same problem as wrecked the novel, in a guise appropriate to poetry. Poetry gives one man's view of the whole world. It is an individual world-view; and therefore needs a social world-view—a highest common factor of all individual world-views—for its communication. The higher the common factor, the richer the communicated view can be. The lack of a social world-view therefore drives the poet to an increasing individualism and locking within himself, an increasing difficulty of expression, or obscurity, and a decreasing public. At the same time, it causes him to make a fetish of the art-work, which more and more becomes the goal of the process.

The novel gives an objective view of a *part* of the world. It is not like the poet's snapshot vision, which includes everything at that instant, with the blurred edges appropriate to a glance at all reality. The novel gives a portion of the world, but gives it from several angles, from several possible individual world-views. The poem is a bunch of perspectives taken from one spot, the "I." The novel is a bunch of perspectives of the "I," or of two or three "I's" taken from every possible spot. One is a field of vision; the other is a viewed thing. The lack of a common world-view, therefore, comes in the novel as the problem of the observer, of the seeing eye, just as the poetic problem emerges as the problem of the world seen. The novel's problem is epistemological, the problem of knowing, of the spectacles through which one sees; the poem is ontological, the problem of being, of the nature of the reality one sees.

All contemporary poets, therefore, who do not dissolve into complete obscurity or vanish into the private world with no public, save themselves from this dissolution only by a desperate attempt to salvage a world-view from the wreck of culture. Such poets as Graves and Davies show a progressive decline as the difficulty gets them in its grip. Housman finds even his highly artificial world-view, based on a pastoral atmosphere of fifty years ago, impossible to maintain except for brief periods of excitement, and he has long been silent. The Sitwells attempt the romantic Keatsian expedient, the selection of words with bright visual or sensual affective tones, drawn from literature and not from contemporary being, and therefore constituting a closed world, glittering and dreamlike. This attempt collapses, because the unreality robs the affective tones of depth and poignancy. The poetry becomes "unfeeling," and the more brightly the colours are piled on, the more they seem unreal and hollow. De la Mare attempts to construct a world-view of the fairy supernatural, but the impossibility of belief in such a world robs it of value. It is not suggested that one must believe in fairies or ghosts to make poetry of them. But one must believe in a world in which they have a definite place, either as things really existing, or as projections of the unconscious, or as myths, or as examples of the absurdity of mankind, or as emanations of the devil. The decaying bourgeois has no definite beliefs about fairies, no positive attitude, only a suspension or mixture of beliefs and a negative attitude. Poetry is not built from negative attitudes. Hence De la Mare has ceased to write poetry. Exactly the same attempt to patch up a world-view occurs with Yeats. This time it is to be composed of theosophy, the Gods, and neo-Platonic philosophy. In spite of Yeats' clear recognition of the absolute necessity of a world-view to the poet, the attempt fails, for what Yeats and all those like him cannot achieve is a *common* world-view. Yeats may by an heroic act of will build up a world-view of definite belief in magic, fairies, the gods and symbols of occult truths, but he cannot ensure that his belief will be present in his contemporaries. On the contrary, he merely adds yet another to the anarchic world-views of current culture. Consequently, his poetry is full of evocative references and allusions which are simply missed by his readers who do not share this world-view, and even the notes he gives do not help.

Eliot is perhaps the best clinical picture of the modern poet's illness. He sees quite clearly that the poet and his readers have no world-view in common, that everyone's faiths, affective associations, hopes and goals are different from every other's. Eliot (and it is noteworthy that like Yeats and the significant contemporary novelists he is an alien) believes that he has discovered a common social world, that of literary tradition. In our reading, in our sharing of experiences with dead authors, we get affective associations to words which should, therefore, be usable as a social medium. *The Waste Land* is a product of this. The literature of several languages and several epochs is ransacked for affective associations, and the present is continually repictured in the colours of past literature. The expedient is not successful except as a unique *tour de force*. The common world-view of literature is in fact an illusion. Unless there is a common world-view of reality, there cannot be a common world-view of literature. Eliot himself proves this by providing an elaborate apparatus of notes, which would not be necessary if all his readers lived in the same literary world. Actually, a note is no substitute for an emotional experience derived from reading an author; for a man to have Eliot's emotional reactions to Dante, the Upanishads, Verlaine, Frazer, Webster, and Australian doggerel ballad he must have not only Eliot's world-view but Eliot's personal experience in literature. Therefore Eliot's theory proves to be illusory. His technique leads to a personal world-view, to obscurity, to the contracting public. He draws upon a *personal* life experience, upon his own experience in reading books, which cannot be experienced by another.

Eliot's thesis has another consequence. Since the modern world is always described in terms of past literature, it is a dead world. It is a walking mummy, a galvanised corpse, decked out in the finery of a forgotten age, strangely mimicking modern gestures. This is inevitable, for it is implicit in the technique, and gives *The Waste Land* so pessimistic, so utterly hopeless a tone; there is no hope when the present abandons itself to the past. This also is just what makes the poem so brilliantly representative of that epoch.

Eliot's theory of poetry raises several problems. Of this the most important is that of belief. If I ransack the cultures of several ages for emotional provender, must I adopt their beliefs?

Eliot's solution is typically bourgeois. The poet's mind is a catalyst. The poem is created inside the mind by the mixture of ideas, and the poet's mind remains throughout neutral and unchanged.

This is the typical bourgeois myth of the free man, the undetermined observer, the man who participates in social process without being affected by it. Even the analogy is fallacious. Any reaction hastened by a catalyst can take place without that particular catalyst, but no one has yet seen poems created without a mind. The theory of ideas and emotions contained in a mind, which remains aloof from them, is as illogical and absurd as a red hot poker in which the iron is aloof from the heat. Thoughts and emotions are states of the mind. How can an object be unchanged by its states, when change is simply alteration of state?

The actual answer to Eliot's problem of belief is this. It is merely the old difficulty of relative truth, and the unity of truth and error. Each hypothesis which represents some aspect of reality contains a measure of truth, and also necessarily a measure of error. One hypothesis can be destroyed only by another containing a greater measure of truth. Moreover, this process of destruction also analyses the older hypothesis, revealing its hitherto unsuspected error as well as its truth; therefore the second statement not only includes the new truth but also the old hypothesis, now analysed into truth and error.

In the same way, in its attitude to beliefs of an older generation—for example to Dantesque scholasticism—our culture sees clearly both Dante's truth and Dante's error. It therefore includes Dantesque faith and the Dantesque world-view, now overt, analysed into its truth and its error, and expressed in terms of our higher faith and larger world-view. Our culture is therefore competent to appreciate Dante's poetry, just as an Einsteinian can appreciate Newton's theories. It is not a case, therefore, of pretending to believe what Dante believed; it is a question of understanding what

= 129 =

his belief was. Then, although we no longer believe in his God: *"In la sua volontade è nostra pace"* is still poetry. It is included in our wider view of reality. It is historic.

But the bourgeois, in ceasing to have that historical world-view today, has ceased to possess a view competent to include that of older cultures. He is ceasing even to have one which will include the disintegrating elements of his own culture; therefore like Eliot he ceaselessly pursues the task of finding one in the past.

Eliot's late attempt was to become, by an effort of faith like that of Yeats, classicist, Royalist, and Anglo-Catholic. It was natural that Eliot, turning to a literary world-view for art, when this failed, should as an alien be unable to seek anything rooted in current social relations, look for another tradition and find it in the English Church. Here was a world-view imposed on all its members, the world-view of the 39 Articles and the Sacraments and theology.

But this unity too is an illusion. Christianity, like every other element in bourgeois culture, is disintegrating into a thousand world-views. The 39 Articles are accepted, but not believed in. The tradition even if alive would only be a reactionary tradition, the world-view of a dying force. But it is already decomposed, and with this act Eliot ceases to be significant as an artist.

Meanwhile a school represented by Auden, Lewis, and Spender, with knowledge of the nature of the problem, unsuccessfully attempts to grapple with it; unsuccessfully, because they do not perfectly see the causes that have brought about the debacle of English poetry, nor what precisely it is that is distorting contemporary ideology. They remain in fact bourgeois revolutionaries.

= 130 =

What is the position of this group and of their followers? Unlike their predecessors, they are perfectly aware of the cause of decay in bourgeois culture—that it is an outworn system of economic relations holding back productive forces—and of its only possible cure, social revolution. But they cannot see either the decay or the revolution in other than bourgeois terms. They still regard themselves as sources of free thought in the bourgeois manner. They still live in personal worlds. They see social relations as fettering them, but they do not see these as determining them. They regard a revolution as the means of removing all those factors that are preventing the free development of human minds, which are regarded as self-determined sources from which issue all energy, which put forth and never take in. They still move within the circle of the individual as benefactor, as producer, as active force, never as beneficiary, consumer, patient. In fine, they cannot see freedom as the consciousness of necessity.

Their philosophy, therefore, is not Communism, but anarchy. All their hopes are drawn from bourgeois culture. Bourgeois social relations constrain the very hopes they produce. They wish these relations broken so as to give outlet to the bourgeois hopes. Thus they accept uncritically nearly all the products of bourgeois ideology—Freudism, Einsteinism, bourgeois psychology, history, aesthetics, conceptions of freedom, peace, love, liberty, and justice. With these they necessarily accept the anarchic world-views of the bourgeois. This fact is reflected in their technique, which betrays a similar obscurity, a plethora of purely personal associations, and an historical irresponsibility as great as that of purely bourgeois poets like Eliot or Cummings. They are trying to attain a universal world-view, which necessarily will be Communist. Consequently, through their obscurity and bourgeois revolutionary anarchy runs a clear thread of certain Communist ideas—the necessity of revolution, the decay of bourgeois culture, the rise of the proletariat. But these ideas are applied mechanically; they are imposed because the poets themselves have merely imposed these ideas on their own bourgeois ideologies, without accepting them. They have not become Communists throughout; they have not transformed, sifted, and synthesised all bourgeois culture, physics, psychology, ethics, and history into a Communist world-view. They are revolting bourgeois anarchists prepared to aid the revolution. They are not yet citizens of the future by conquest, as a bourgeois might become, nor born citizens of the future, as a proletarian might already be.

Their attitude on two points is symptomatic. One is their attitude towards Soviet Russia. It is, at any rate with Lewis and Spender, entirely an anxious solicitude about the freedom of the writer, a worry as to whether or not there is censorship and to what extent. This shows that the lesson of the complete and disastrous collapse of "free" bourgeois literature in our age has been without meaning to them. They still believe in the free artist, undetermined by social relations. They still suppose that art, as an activity, can exist apart from social activity. They do not accept that whatever methods are necessary for a social transformation must be necessary in art, and that, if it is in fact essential for the progress of society, its process must be consciously known and controlled, this applies to art, as well as to hat-making. We have sufficiently examined this error and its consequences elsewhere, and all that it is necessary to say here is that anyone who retains such an illusion remains a bourgeois, even though he revolts against bourgeoisdom.

Secondly, there is their attitude towards the role of the artist in a revolutionary situation. They appreciate that the artist must be revolutionary, that bourgeois relations are a source of decay, but at the same time they insist that the artist must be free as revolutionary, that he must be a "free" source of revolutionary energy. They therefore proceed to betray art, simply because they remain bourgeois, by their conception of the revolutionary artist *as agitator*.

It is true that every human being—bourgeois or proletarian, writer, scientist, or schoolteacher, busman or miner—who has attained an understanding of the present situation must become a revolutionary. But to be a revolutionary means that you must will a revolution, and to will a revolution means that you must understand how it is brought about. You must grasp the technique of revolution, which is rooted in the revolutionary situation as it is today. You must therefore grasp the Marxist-Leninist analysis of the process of revolution, and understand that a proletarian revolution does not come from above, that it is not the result of ideas imposed by individuals or preached by enthusiastic poets, but that it is a class movement springing from the pressure of the economic forces of the time. In this movement Marxists certainly play the role of leaders, not leaders from another class, but leaders as members of the energetic class. The Communist Party leads a revolutionary movement, but it leads it as the conscious portion of a class; it makes conscious, and gives a political shape to, the aspirations and desires of that class, not to aspirations or desires imposed upon that class. It shows, patiently and carefully, the only way in which those desires may be realised, and points out the contradictions and impracticability of other methods. It does not itself implant those desires. It must identify itself with the revolting class; as a leader it must remain solid with those whom it expects to follow it. Any other theory of revolution is unreal, and can result only in a change in the form, not the reality, of government.

If the world is to be changed, if an end is to be achieved, it is like building a ship, though a vaster task. It requires the cooperation of the builders. The task itself imposes discipline, unity, and determinism of labour on those who participate in it. It is not possible to work a factory individualistically, but either dominatingly (as is capitalism or slave-owning) or cooperatively (as in Communism). A Communist revolution must be cooperative, and a revolutionary must accept the determination of his task imposed by the common task.

The plan of the ship imposes the positions of the men, their number, their actions, and their movement. The plan of the canal and the lie of the country through which it passes, determines the earth to be shifted, what men are sent here, what there; the tactics of each stage are dictated by the nature of the task. The tactics can be mistaken, because an engineer may make a slip in an estimate; a surveyor may be guilty of incorrect mensuration; a geologist may be wrong about the presence of rock; a foreman may insert too large a charge of dynamite. But in the nature of the case, only one correct tactic is possible, and this is the product, not of men's will as such, but of reality as perceived by men. This applies just as adequately to the task of revolution and reconstruction. A revolutionary must be a member of the revolutionary party.

He must participate in its problems and help to form its tactics. He must execute the plans it has formed and which he had helped to form. He must cooperate in settling, and then accept and implement, the *party line*. He must work loyally inside his group, and perform his small or large share of the common plan. As long as he remains outside this revolutionary party, it is a sign that although he believes in the need for a revolution he remains bourgeois.

The conception of the poet as agitator springs from this view. Such a man conceives the artist, quite in the bourgeois manner, to be a free source of energy, helping to bring about the revolution by imposing ideas upon it in an attractive dress, according to his own view of Utopia and his own private values.

Such agitational poetry cannot be great poetry, because it springs from a divided world-view. It has an obscure bourgeois basis, on which is imposed a mechanical pseudo-Marxist revolutionary formula. It sometimes has quite an unpleasant air, as of a bourgeois trying to "cash in" on the revolution. Such poets are in grave danger of being unconscious parasites on the revolution, of letting others do the work and themselves reaping the grain. Of course they cannot in fact achieve this; the grain can be reaped only by those who sow it.

What, then, is the proper position for a bourgeois poet today who finds himself arrived at the situation of Auden, Spender, and Lewis? To be a revolutionary, certainly, but a real revolutionary, not a free-lance agitator; to be a member of a revolutionary party and to carry out a common party line, not his own line; to be a revolutionary not only in blank verse but in every activity which he can carry out and his party suggests. Agitation is necessary certainly, so is propaganda, but

= 135 =

let the poet be a genuine propagandist, not a blank-verse propagandist. Is the proletariat made conscious of its goal by rhymed economics? No, verse is not, and never was, the instrument of propaganda in this sense. The class that is to be made conscious of its mission must be shown this directly and concretely, in terms of an analysis of its situation at a given time in simple words, in terms of unemployment, war, fascism, imperialism, victimisation, and profiteering. It must grow from the concrete situation with which the persons addressed are faced, whether they are trade unionists, mothers, soldiers, or unemployed. It must discuss those problems which they feel immediately and directly pressing upon them; this is not opportunism, because the discussion is based on a clear Marxist world-view, which is just what Auden, Spender, and Lewis lack.

The dissolution of bourgeois culture involves, as we saw, a reduction in poetry's public and an increasingly private world-view for the individual poet. This situation can be altered only by changing the world. But to try to change the world by operation entirely within the tiny group formed by the dissolution of bourgeois culture—the poetic public—is like trying to pull a house down by dragging at the smoke from the chimney. Notice that not only does this attempt not revitalise poetry, but it gives rise to a perversion of poetry, self-consciously propagandist poetry. Poetry can be revitalised only by a change of the economic relations on which it rests, and a corresponding change and synthesis of the dissolving culture of today.

Does this mean that the poets must stop writing poetry until the new order comes into being as a result of their non-poetic efforts? Not altogether. Nothing stands still, and as the old order changes into the

= 136 =

new (is even now so changing), the poet can success-fully endeavor to change poetry, to make it social and public again. But a prerequisite is to attain a world-view that will become general. He can attain such a view only by destructively analysing all bourgeois cul-ture, separating the best elements, synthesising them, and advancing to a new world-view—in a word by be-coming a thorough Marxist and not merely acquiring a Marxist façade. This, Auden, Spender, and Lewis have so far failed to do. This book itself would really be a poet's task—a small attempt towards the creation of such a world-view, at present limited to only a few, but one which will, as culture advances, become the general world-view of culture, and as a result become far richer and subtler. Having achieved that world-view, the poet, when he has a new experience that necessitates expression in poetry, can then project it into the new world struggling to be born and become a poet of the future. But this requires the destructive analysis and synthesis of bourgeois culture, itself a revolutionary task. Auden, Lewis, and Spender attempt to skip this essential transition, and therefore fall back into the old dying world.

Against this negative role, there is their positive part. This must not be overlooked. In its fight against capitalism, the proletariat needs all helpers; to its standard rally all those bourgeois disgusted or crippled by the world they have made. Anarchists as well as Communists combine to pull down the old world. Pacifists as well as Communists unite to make an end of war. Sincere Christians as well as dialectical mate-rialists attack these conditions which outrage all sys-tems of morals and all ideals. All bourgeois scientists, artists, and intellectuals revolt against a system that fetters science, art, and intellect. Nationalists as well as creators of a classless world fight against the finance capital that enslaves and destroys all national cultures. The leadership and the mass basis can come only from the proletariat, but all bourgeois revolutionaries, valuable and important auxiliaries, conscious that these things must perish from the earth, march with them in demonstrations, are solid with them in resistance, and assist them to fulfil their task at last, and advance to a new world.

The task of construction which follows can be performed adequately only by real Communists, for it is Communism that is being built. The task transforms the man; the dyer's hand is subdued to what it works in. The task of socialist construction enables bourgeois revolutionaries to transform themselves, to shed their illusions and their superstitions, and become Communists. These fellow-travellers become fellow-citizens. Auden, Spender, and Lewis are young, sincere, and intelligent, and they will escape from the bourgeois round; they will become complete Communists and help to create a new vital poetry, instead of galvanising with mechanical formulae a dead body.

. . . . .

THIS ENDS, then, our survey of English bourgeois literature. Necessarily brief, it has confined itself to the tracing of those chief social changes which produced change in the form and technique of the novel and poetry. This fundamental change occurs at the economic level. Does this mean that to a Marxist the study of literature is a branch of economics? By no means, but it means that literature is determined by social forces, by the movement of the society that secretes it, just as the sea is determined in its shape by the land, in its surface by the wind, in its depth by the

= 138 =

sea bed, in its volume by the ingress of river water and rain and the egress of water vapour, and yet remains distinctively the sea, saline, liquid, marine.

It is the bourgeois error to believe in the existence of self-determined spheres of phenomena—physics, biology, aesthetics, morals, and philosophy. It is a bourgeois error, arising from the first to suppose *either* that these spheres are closed and self-determined *or* that the laws of one sphere (physics, morals, etc.) must determine all spheres completely. In fact, distinguishable spheres exist and these spheres mutually determine each other, and are in complete relation to each other, like a river and its bed.

Thus the study of aesthetics includes the appreciation of primarily aesthetic values detected in the tasting and the creation, in values of beauty, emotion, colour, and life. Such a study is beyond the scope of this book. To deal fully and appreciatively with these values in one author alone would perhaps occupy several books. In addition there are the laws, given in the social situation, whereby both the tasting and the creation are conditioned. These laws determine the experience of the genotypes of reader and writer in society. This sphere also is complex, and it is this study which, in a very brief way, has been the aim pursued above. We cannot neglect such a study if we are to enrich and expand our values, and escape from the barren categories of the present. If we live within a culture, breathing its air and sharing its coherent world-view, such an analysis need form no part of aesthetics, for the results of such an analysis are given in our own experience. We share the common world-view. But when a culture disintegrates, when we lose a world-view, then aesthetics too disintegrates: our values, which seemed so clear, so much part of the art-work, abruptly fade. To restore them, to advance beyond, to create a new art or new world-view, a new set of aesthetic values, a new life, is the purpose now of any analysis of the social generation of art. It then becomes an essential preliminary task for the recreation of art and aesthetics.

INDEX